The Anglican Way:
Evangelical and Catholic

D1553338

The Anglican Way

Evangelical and Catholic

by

Peter Toon

Morehouse-Barlow Co., Inc.
Wilton, Connecticut 06897

Morehouse-Barlow Co., Inc.
78 Danbury Road
Wilton, Connecticut 06897

ISBN 0-8192-1330-6

Library of Congress Catalog Card Number 83-60934

Printed in the United States of America

For
Rudy and Mildred
Jeffrey and Debra
four good American friends

I was born in England and the Church of England is still an established Church. But, nevertheless, I am a convert to that Church and thus to the principles of Anglicanism. It is said that converts are often the most enthusiastic members. Perhaps this is so.

In this short book I certainly write enthusiastically to offer both to my fellow Anglicans, as well as to my fellow Christians called by other names, that which I see as the calling of God to Anglicanism (and specifically to the American Episcopal Church). By what right do I share my vision with my American brothers and sisters in Christ? I have no right but I do care for the Episcopal Church and I do look forward to my visits to the United States in order to preach, teach and enjoy fellowship.

This book is not specifically for scholars but for concerned Anglicans (and friends of Anglicanism) who long for spiritual, theological and moral renewal. I have not provided footnotes for it is not the details but the general structure of the contents that is important. I have been like a busy bee collecting ideas from a variety of places but the result (I hope it is as sweet as honey) is my own provision. The vision I describe is what I see.

The writing has been done while suffering from a broken right wrist and so it has been more a dictating than a writing exercise. My wife has kindly typed out my material and so again I am indebted to her.

Lent 1983

Peter Toon
The Rectory, Boxford
Suffolk, England

1

God's Call

There are many Christian denominations in North America. Each one claims to be part of the one, holy, catholic and apostolic Church of God. Each one seeks to be loyal to Jesus of Nazareth as Saviour and Lord. Yet each one is different from the others. For example, most of us are aware of the great differences between the Roman Catholic Church and the Southern Baptist Convention of churches. But only those who are closely involved know the subtle differences between one kind of Baptist group and another.

This book is not about differences between denominations. It is about the Episcopal Church of the United States (or any Anglican Church anywhere in the world). The Episcopal Church is a member of the family of Anglican Churches whose mother Church is that centered on Canterbury, England. This book is not a history of the Episcopal Church or a statement of its doctrines. Rather, it is the presentation of an attractive and compelling way of understanding the distinctive claim that can, and should, be made for the Episcopal Church.

In one sentence, the claim is that the Episcopal Church is called to be both evangelical and catholic. In other words, the call of God to the Episcopal Church in these times, when the one Church of God is sadly divided, is that it should be simultaneously evangelical and catholic. This does not mean that she is to be evangelical in her preaching and catholic in her liturgy. It is not a matter of being sometimes evangelical and sometimes catholic. The Church is called to be catholic and evangelical all the time in all that she is and does.

Perhaps a simple illustration will help. A typical football team is both wholly male and from one college. The team performs best when it plays in the strength and vigor of its masculinity and also for the love and honor of the college. Masculine strength and skill if not properly motivated and guided by the unity that loyalty to the college creates will achieve little. And united effort for the college without the power of fit and skillful men in the team will not produce good and successful football. Masculine vigor and unity go together before and during the match.

Now there is no country on earth where there is more talk of the Gospel (= Evangel) than in America. Many Christians call themselves evangelicals in order to make the claim of the priority of the Evangel in their faith and practice known. Publishing houses produce hundreds of books each year commending and explaining the Gospel. Radio and television stations bring gospel-messages and singing into thousands of homes. Associations and societies exist by the dozen for the protection and propagation of the Gospel. America, we must conclude, is not short of talk and activity on behalf of the Evangel of Jesus Christ.

But few of these millions who say they are committed to the Evangel pay much attention to what I shall call Catholicity. The majority of evangelicals do not think of the wholeness of the one Church in space and time. The beauty of Liturgy, the symbolic power of sacraments, the depth of spirituality, and the episcopate as a sign of unity, are themes which rarely enter their minds except in a negative way. They tend to think and act as if there were no Church of God from the time when the New Testament was written until the modern era when their own particular group came into existence. This way of thinking is like that of the person who, in tracing the family tree, does not want to know about a long section in it, because the members of the family in those years were not pleasing to him.

It is easy to criticize evangelicals but they are not the only offenders. If they are guilty of neglecting important truths about the Church as catholic then others are guilty of neglecting the Gospel, which is the treasure of the Church. Regrettably, it is often the case in much Anglican practice (and the same applies to Roman Catholics and others) that the treasure of the Gospel is lost somewhere in thick layers of tradition which reach back into the dim past. Power and glory are lost in archaeological religion. The situation here is like that of the woman who kept on peeling the onion until there was nothing left in hand; only a pile of layers of onion on the table.

The contention of this book is that the particular history of the Anglican (Episcopal) Church together with its approach to liturgy, ordained ministry and doctrine require, and call it to be, wholly evangelical and wholly catholic. If it does not express this duality all the time it is failing. God's call to the Episcopal Church and Anglicanism is that it should exhibit simultaneously commitment to Gospel and Catholicity.

It is possible to be evangelical and effectively to disown Christ. It is possible to be catholic-minded and effectively to betray Christ. This is possible, and this in fact happens, because either a system of doctrines or a system of ritual becomes primary in Christian experience. Even as Marxists are committed to an ideology, so religious people may be committed to an ideology — a system of beliefs — in such a way that this system is their basic interest and primary commitment. The personal relationship to Jesus Christ is thereby eclipsed or made ineffectual. Much the same applies to an excessive commitment to ritualism and ceremonial. Here persons are so involved with the apparatus, structure, and functioning of things that they miss the divine Reality behind the appearances. There is little possibility, therefore, for a dynamic relationship with Jesus Christ because a false barrier exists to prevent such a relationship.

To say this is not to say that commitment to the Gospel and commitment to Catholicity are wrong. It is to say, rather, that both only take on their true meaning and function when they are in the right relationship to Jesus Christ; or, put another way, when the Christian, who is in a right relationship to Jesus Christ, knows how each of them should function in his experience and faith. There must always be the primacy of Jesus Christ, who is the same yesterday, today, and forever. Without him there is no Gospel and without him there is no Catholicity. The Gospel exists and is proclaimed because he not only rose from the dead but ascended into heaven to sit at the Father's right hand, from where he sent the Holy Spirit to be his representative on earth. He is the Lord of the Church; it is he who not only guides and rules the Church but who also gives the Church spiritual life. He is the One who provides the gifts of the Spirit to all believers, according to the wisdom of God. He is the One who is present at, and in, every sacrament. It is Christ who presides at the Holy Communion and gives the food of his own crucified and now glorified body; it is Christ who acts in every baptismal service giving his Spirit to the one who is baptized and making that person a member of his spiritual body, the Church.

So we see that without Christ there is no Gospel and without

Christ there is no meaning to the experience and history of the Church throughout the centuries. This is not to say that the Gospel has always been rightly preached and rightly understood. And it is not to say that the Church in history has always been correct in what it has said and done, or failed to say and failed to do. But what we must believe is that Christ is the One who brought into existence the Gospel of God and Christ is the One without whom there is no Church and cannot be any Church. What we have to guard against is the rejection of either the achievement of Christ in creating the Gospel or the continuing achievement of Christ in ruling and directing the Church throughout history. On the one side, there are those who, looking at the painful history of the Church through the years, feel that the Church has made so many mistakes and gone wrong so often, they want to pay no attention to the accumulated experience which belongs to the historical pilgrimage of the Church throughout the centuries. On the other side, there are those who, noting that those who claim to be gospel-centered speak with so many voices, take refuge in the Church as it has developed through the centuries. Here the Church is seen as the bulwark of the truth and this means that the person finds a kind of refuge in its structures, liturgy, authority, canon law and the ordained ministry. In this, the person feels safe and so engages wholeheartedly in the activities of religion, and may do so with little or no attention to the achievement of Jesus Christ in the creation of the Gospel of God.

On the one side, Jesus Christ is seen as tremendously active in the creation of the Gospel and the foundation of the Church; yet he is dismissed as basically 'inactive' throughout the centuries until the birth of Protestantism in the sixteenth century (or even to the birth of modern denominations in the nineteenth and twentieth centuries). On the other side, Christ is seen as active throughout history guiding the Church from the first through to the present century, but he is not wholly recognized as the One who created the Gospel and is ever concerned to renew the Church by the Gospel. These two sides are the two extremes of the pendulum and in what they positively affirm they are right. Of course Christ created the Gospel: of course Christ ruled and rules the Church. What we do not want is merely one swing of the pendulum in one direction or the other. We want the whole movement of the pendulum swinging in both directions and covering all space between each extreme; we want to be committed to the Evangel and to Catholicity. We want the Christ who created the Gospel as well as the same Christ who has ruled and rules the Church today.

In an earlier book of mine, *God's Church for Today* (1979), I suggested that one model for understanding the Church, was to think of it as looking simultaneously in four directions. Looking upward toward God in faith and worship, looking forward in hope toward the Second Coming of our Lord Jesus Christ and the life of the age to come, looking backward toward the cross and resurrection of Christ and the history of the Church through space and time, and finally looking around upon the needy world and thus engaging in evangelism and social service and mission. What I wrote then I still endorse today; but what I shall do in this book is to present a definite picture of Anglicanism as called by God, in these days when there is much talk of Church unity, to set an example for the world-wide Church in terms of her simultaneous commitment to the Evangel and to Catholicity. I do not, in any way, want to unchurch members of other denominations and groups, but I do want to call Episcopalians (Anglicans) to the full realization of what their God-given position in Christendom should mean today. Without appearing to be arrogant, I would want to say that, just as ancient Israel was set by God to be a light to the nations, so I see the Anglican Communion of Churches set by God, in the midst of all the Churches, to be a light — providing a luminous example of simultaneous commitment to the Gospel and to Catholicity.

2

The Exalted Christ

The Church is the Church of God the Father; but the Church is built upon and around the Lord Jesus. St. Paul described Christ as the chief cornerstone (Eph. 2:20) — the stone which was strategic and fundamental in terms of the correct alignment and construction of the whole building. The same apostle further declared that the Church is the temple of the Holy Spirit (1 Cor. 3:16), replacing the stone temple of Jerusalem; it is the worshipping community in whom dwells the Spirit of the Lord Jesus.

The Gospel is the Gospel of God the Father; but it is the Gospel concerning his Son, the Lord Jesus. Without Jesus, the Incarnate Son of God, and his saving work on the Cross of Calvary and in bodily resurrection there would be no Gospel. And, that Gospel would not be effective without the Holy Spirit who enables human beings to receive the good news and believe in the Lord Jesus. The truth is that no human being can say that Jesus is Lord except with the help of the Holy Spirit.

Therefore neither the Church nor the Gospel could exist and have meaning except in their relation to God, who is Father, Son, and Holy Spirit.

It is of particular importance that we have a clear view of the present position of the Lord Jesus for he is the mediator between God and mankind. But first we need to recall his sacrificial death and wonderful resurrection from that death. Paul wrote:

> I passed on to you what I received, which is of the greatest importance: that Christ died for our sins, as written in the Scriptures; that he was buried and that he was raised to life three days later, as written in the scriptures (1 Cor. 15:3–4).

This is Paul's summary of the facts of the Gospel.

The essence of the proclamation of the apostles and first Chris-

tians appears to have been: 'We proclaim good news of God's
salvation in and through the crucified and risen Lord Jesus.'
Sometimes the death of Jesus was emphasized, and sometimes
the resurrection was stressed; but, the two belonged inseparably
together. The Gospel centered on the risen (ascended) Lord who
had been crucified. Let us look at 1 Corinthians 15:3–5 more
closely.

Christ died for our sins as written in the Scriptures. The manner
of death is not described; merely the fact of death is stated. It
was the death of the Messiah 'for our sins' (i.e. for the forgiveness, eradication and cleansing of our sins). The death is presented as a vicarious, or representative, or substitionary sacrifice.
As such it was described by Isaiah (52:13–53:12) and in Psalm
22.

He was buried. Jesus was truly dead; from the strictest medical
point of view, he died.

*He was raised to life three days later as written in the Scrip-
tures.* The reality of the resurrection is emphasized and the Old
Testament prophecies of the vindication of God's righteous servant, the Messiah, (Isaiah 53) are noted. In the following verses
(verses 6–11) a list of people who saw the risen Jesus is provided.

In this passage two of the verbs are in the aorist tense, the
tense which denotes past completed action (i.e. he died; he was
buried). But the 'was raised' in verse 4 is in the perfect tense, a
tense often used to point to the ongoing influence of a past event
in the present. So Jesus is presented by Paul not only as raised
from death, but also as the Lord of the present. The ascension is
implied by the resurrection and it is in the living Christ that we
now find salvation and life.

Thus it may be said that in these verses Paul provided a whole
Gospel, giving due emphasis to the two inseparables—the death
and resurrection (with ascension) of Jesus. On Good Friday we
think primarily of the death; on Easter Day we think primarily of
the Resurrection. But the Gospel is about the risen Lord who has
been crucified.

Crucified God

The eternal Father sent the eternal Son into our space and time
to become the son of Mary, a young Jewish virgin, and to be
called Jesus. The theological understanding of the virginal conception (or, less precisely, the virginal birth) of Jesus may be set

out briefly as follows. First, the fact that Mary was a virgin points to the fact that the conception of Jesus was wholly the result of the divine initiative, the work of the Holy Spirit; he had no human father. Secondly, the fact that he had no earthly father means that his existence in space and time causes us to look into no time (eternity) and no space (infinity) for the truth concerning him; that is, to his eternal origin in the life of the Holy Trinity. He is truly a human being, but more than a mere man: for 'the Word became flesh and dwelt among us, full of grace and truth' (John 1:14). Thirdly, the virginal conception testifies that he who was born of Mary was not a new person. When a child is conceived in the normal manner he or she is a new individual. Mother and father share in God's creative act to make a new and a third person; but, the Person (Gk. *hypostasis;* Lat. *persona*) of the eternal Son of God took to himself a human nature which he gained from Mary, the virgin. He exists eternally with his divine nature, but from a given point and moment in space and time he also exists with our human nature.

Jesus of Nazareth was put to death on a cross outside the city walls of ancient Jerusalem. Crucifixion was a Roman form of execution used chiefly for slaves. It was a degrading way to die and was never used for Roman citizens. Cicero, the great defender of classical culture and civilization, regarded this form of execution as barbaric. He wrote:

Should death be threatening, then we want to die in freedom; The executioner, the shrouding of the head and the mere mention of the cross must all be banished not only from the lips of Roman citizens, but also from their thoughts, eyes and ears.

Josephus, the Jewish historian, described it as 'the most wretched of all ways of dying.' Crucifixion and civilization did not belong together. Educated Roman and pious Jew alike regarded it with horror and shame. It was an extremely degrading, painful, and cruel form of death—the grossest, cruelest, and most hideous manner of execution.

Jesus died on a cross. In terms of the best Roman and Jewish culture and morality this fact should have been an acute embarrassment to the followers of Jesus. It ought to have been something which they wanted to erase from their memory and certainly never discuss with either friend or foe. Yet, amazingly and remarkably, the opposite happened. So the apostle Paul wrote:

For the word of the cross is folly to those who are perishing
but to us who are being saved it is the power of God.
We preach Christ crucified, a stumbling block to Jews and
folly to Gentiles, but to those who are called, both Jews
and Greeks, Christ the power of God and the wisdom of
God (1 Cor. 1:18 & 23–25).

God made the sign of degradation, barbarism and cruelty the sign
of salvation. So the verse of the hymn by Charles Wesley:

O Love Divine! What hast Thou done?
The immortal God hath died for me!
The Father's co-eternal Son,
Bore all my sin upon the tree,
The Immortal God for me hath died!
My Lord, my Love is crucified.

Likewise every cross and every crucifix testifies to the fact that
God brought hope out of desolation and salvation out of degradation.

The conviction that Christ spent the interval, between expiring
on the Cross and his Resurrection, in the underworld (hades) was
very common in the Church of the first four centuries. Thus the
Creed: 'He descended into hell/hades'.

Two types of interpretation were common among the early
fathers. One was to see the spirit of Jesus proclaiming the Gospel
to the dead in the underworld so that they could believe and
receive eternal life. The other was to portray Jesus as going straight
to hell to do battle with Satan and his evil angels in order truly
to conquer them. In both interpretations is the theme of Christ
the Victor over death and sin, and the two are not mutually ex-
clusive so that it was possible to hold both interpretations. All
the fathers believed that the eternal Son of God, with his human
spirit and personality, was active between his physical death and
bodily resurrection and his activity was a part of his redeeming
work. It was their theology of Holy Saturday.

Although the patristic interpretations have always had support-
ers in the Church, there is a greater tendency in modern times to
interpret the descent in a passive rather than an active way. This
can be done by emphasizing that Jesus truly died; he truly en-
dured the human lot of death in its fullness, solitude and inactivity. 'He descended into hades' means that he entered into the
full reality of death. He fully accepted death and knew its total
power in order to have solidarity with us in and beyond death.

This type of interpretation can be strengthened by stating that to descend into hell, rather than merely into hades, means to feel the full force of God's wrath against sin and to be made a curse for us. It is to die as the substitute and to be punished by God for our sins and wickedness. Thus it is not only the solitude and inactivity of death; it is also the pain and the horror of death.

Resurrected Lord

There were no witnesses of the Resurrection of Jesus. His rising from the dead was seen by no one. What people witnessed was the appearance of the resurrected Jesus; also they saw the empty tomb. In fact only the disciples were witnesses of the appearance of Jesus but disciples and others saw the empty tomb.

Today there is a readiness in the Church to discount or hold loosely to the fact of the Resurrection as an event within history. This tendency must be resisted, for if the Resurrection is not an event within history (within the same physical universe and space and time in which we live) then what God accomplished on the cross in Christ for our salvation is not applicable to us in history. The bodily resurrection is of fundamental importance and as such cannot be ignored, forgotten or cast aside.

As a real event in history, the Resurrection cannot, however, be wholly explained in terms of historical causation. There is both continuity and discontinuity with history. The continuity appears in such facts as the empty tomb, the total disappearance of the dead body, the complete change in the disciples who claimed to have seen Jesus alive, and the sober nature of the narratives in the four Gospels. The discontinuity is in terms of what the believer accepts—the disclosure of the kingdom of God; the incursion of the new creation into the old creation; the foundation of a new humanity in Christ, the second Adam; the disclosure of the power and love of God; the focal point of the relation of the temporal and the eternal, and that Jesus is alive today. Therefore the resurrection of Jesus is beyond history for what God achieved is not open to investigation but is known through revelation, and faith.

Obviously there were both differences and similarities between Jesus before his crucifixion and Jesus after his resurrection. Yet there was a basic identity. Bodily resurrection means resuscitation with transformation. Not only resuscitation (as with Lazarus in John 11) but also the metamorphosis of the body so that there is an identity-in-transformation. The total body of Jesus of Nazareth was wholly changed by the power of God into a non-physical, spiritual body.

Ascended Saviour

Resurrection was followed by ascension into heaven. Jesus went from the human place on earth into God's place in heaven. His ascension was not a journey into outer space, but was rather a removal from space and time into the immediate sphere of God's holy presence. Entering the presence of the Father, Jesus was made to sit at his right hand, which is a way of saying that as the Incarnate Son, he shared in the universal power and reign of the Father. He was also, with his human nature, given the name Lord, the name by which God was known in the Old Testament.

So the present position of our Lord Jesus Christ is that he is in heaven possessing our perfected, glorified human nature, and that as the Incarnate Son of God he shares in the sovereign rule of God the Father. "He became man," or, as we say, he descended from heaven, in order to be Saviour of the world. Therefore, in life, death, resurrection, ascension, he acted as the representative and the substitute of all human beings. As the ascended and living Lord in heaven he continues to function today as our representative and substitute.

It is common in Christian tradition to refer to the exalted Lord Jesus as our Prophet, Priest, and King. This is a way of describing how the Lord Jesus presently acts on behalf of the human race and, in particular, of those who are united to him by faith through the agency of the Spirit. The Father sent the Holy Spirit to the disciples of Jesus (Acts 2). The Spirit came to them bearing the name and the characteristics of Jesus so that, as he indwelt their hearts, his purpose was to guide and lead them into the mind and way of Christ himself. The Church led by the Spirit of Christ is to do the will of God in the way Jesus did the will of God. It is to carry out the mission of Christ in the world as Christ wants the work to be carried out. It is to live in relationship with God and with human beings in the way which Jesus Christ did when he was on earth. Without Christ and the Holy Spirit, who represents Christ on earth, there is no hope for the Church in the world.

Christ, as the exalted Prophet of God, desires to proclaim the

Gospel of God to the whole world. The only way he can do this now is to speak through members of the Church. So he gives spiritual gifts to members of the Church so that some are called to be evangelists and some to be pastors and teachers. And to all his people he gives the desire to share their faith with other people. So Christ the Prophet, the declarer of the good news, preaches to the world in a variety of languages and forms, using the members of his Church whom he enables by the power of the Holy Spirit. Further, as our exalted Prophet, he proclaims God's word within the people of God. He gives gifts to the Church so that individuals within the Church are teachers, exhorters, and guides of Christian faith and understanding. The sermon each Sunday, the teaching in the Sunday School, and the messages of the leaders of the Church should be inspired by Christ, the Prophet, and should be words from God, offered and proclaimed in the name of Christ, by the power of the Holy Spirit.

Christ is our exalted Priest. This is one of the great themes of the Letter to the Hebrews. When he died on the Cross, Jesus achieved two simultaneous ends. As the Priest of God he offered a full, sufficient sacrifice for the sins of the whole world; yet, the offering that he made was himself, a perfect human being without sin. In his ascension we are to think of Jesus taking that sacrifice (that is, taking himself) into the presence of God, so that there is now in heaven itself, ever before the gaze of the heavenly Father, that Sacrifice which takes away the sins of the world. Yet, that Sacrifice is the living Lord Jesus Christ, who also functions as a Priest in that he presents the Church, its work, its worship, and its prayers to God the Father so that they are acceptable to him. On earth the Church of God serves and worships the Lord in the power of the Holy Spirit and this service, work and worship is offered to the Father in the name of Jesus Christ. Because it is offered in his name, and passes through him to the Father, it is caught up within his constant worship of, and communion with, the Father and is thereby perfected. Without the presence of Christ, our Priest in heaven, and the indwelling Spirit on earth, the worship and prayer of the Church on earth would be a waste of time. Those who respond to the Gospel of God, by believing in our Lord Jesus Christ, are only able to be saved, to receive God's forgiveness and acceptance, because they come to God in the power of the Holy Spirit through Christ, the Priest. Christ draws men and women to himself by the Spirit as the Gospel is preached in the power of the Holy Spirit, and, drawing people to himself, he thereby presents them to the Father to be accepted as the children of God.

The exalted Lord Jesus is also the King. This is another way of expressing the early Christian conviction that 'Jesus Christ is Lord'. It means that sharing in the universal rule of the cosmos by the Father, Jesus Christ is able to guide events on earth for the good of the Church. It means also that he is the Head and Ruler and Source of life for the Church. He rules the Church from heaven and through the Holy Spirit exercises that rule in those who function as pastors and leaders of the Church on earth. And he is not a King and Lord who merely gives orders from afar; but, what he requires to be done, he also enables to be done because he is the One who sends the Holy Spirit to help, assist and provide the necessary spiritual gifts for human beings to obey the will of God. The exalted Jesus is not sometimes Prophet, and at other times Priest or King. He is always and for evermore our Prophet, Priest and King.

So we are to think of our Lord Jesus Christ, through the imagery which the Bible and the Creeds provide, as both the eternal Son of God and the perfected and glorified Man. He is the eternal Son of God with our human nature; he is the Incarnate Son. Thus he is the perfect mediator between God and the human race. Having lived our life and experienced death on our behalf, he is now in heaven to represent his people, and, it is from him that the Church receives both its direction and its power.

The Church of God and her mission in the world wholly depend upon the Lordship of Jesus Christ, and of the presence on earth of the Spirit of Christ with the people of God. The Church without her Lord, and the Church without the Spirit of her Lord, is just another human organization and society, standing alongside countless other human groupings. The Church exists because of her Lord, and exists with her Lord for her Lord. The Church was brought into being by the Gospel concerning her Lord and the Church exists to live by, to exemplify, and to proclaim that same Gospel of her Lord. Only as the Church is in spiritual union and communion with her exalted Lord through the Holy Spirit can she truly be Evangelical and Catholic at all times and in all circumstances.

Though there is an equality of divinity in Father, Son, and Holy Spirit, the way in which they relate to us, as one God, in our salvation is to be noted. The origin of salvation is with the grace and will of the Father; Jesus Christ, as the Incarnate Son of God, is the One who makes our salvation a possibility; and it is the Holy Spirit who then creates within us, as individuals and corporately as a fellowship, that salvation which Christ has achieved for us. So when we think about the Church and the Gospel we must think first of Jesus Christ before we think of the work of the Spirit of God, who comes to us in the name of Christ and bearing the characteristics of Christ. Many parishes have benefited from the Charismatic Movement. There has been a tendency in this movement to think too much about the indwelling Holy Spirit and not sufficiently about the exalted Lord Jesus. We must bear in mind the way in which God has himself revealed himself to us in his saving work and allow our minds first to dwell upon Jesus Christ, our exalted Prophet, Priest, and King, and then from him, and through him, to allow our minds to think of the Holy Spirit who comes to us in Christ's name, bearing the virtues and characteristics of Christ. In this way we shall truly follow the divinely revealed and ordained way of our salvation.

And let us not forget what the Creed affirms: 'Christ . . . is seated at the right hand of God the Father almighty; from there he shall come to judge the living and the dead.' The Church's hope is centered on the personal return to earth, into our space and time, of our exalted Lord.

PART 1

The Evangel

3

By Grace Alone

Have you been accosted by an enthusiast who asks you, 'Are you saved?' Maybe you have a standard reply, or perhaps you don't know what to say. If you are a baptized Christian then you ought to say: 'In Christ Jesus my salvation is completed and complete; because of the indwelling Spirit in my heart I am in the process of being saved; and, because Jesus Christ rose from the dead and will return from heaven at the end of the age to raise the dead, I look forward to salvation at the end of the age.' That is perhaps a long answer but it is a right answer. Salvation is a large idea; it cannot be reduced either to past, or present, or future, for it includes all three.

The Gospel is of God's salvation (Eph. 1:13). In the New Testament the Gospel is called the good news of, and from, God (Mark 1:14) and good news of Jesus Christ who brought it and embodied it in the world (Mark 1:1). It is good news of truth concerning the present and ultimate meaning of life (Gal. 2:5, 14), good news of peace and reconciliation with God and his creation (Eph. 6:15) and of a richness of life which begins now and reaches its fullness through death in the age of the life to come (2 Tim. 1:10). The good news is so important that for it we must risk everything (Mark 8:35; 10:29). Like all good things, the good news can be missed or refused (Rom. 2:16; 10:16), and it can, regrettably, be twisted and distorted by ignorant or unscrupulous people (Gal. 1:6–7).

Salvation

It was easier for the Church in earlier centuries to communicate God's salvation than it is for us today in western society. If we think of either the early centuries after the ascension of Christ, or the more recent centuries since the Protestant Reformation, the situation is much the same. There were high levels of infant mortality; people were considered old at forty; brutality was accepted within the veneer of civilization; very little if anything, could be done about many types of human suffering; there was a general sense of the inevitability of difficulties and problems, often coupled with a sense of fatalism, and there was a general yearning for a state in which there would be relief from all the problems, difficulties and disasters of life.

If you contrast this state of affairs with those we experience in modern western society, then you can see the point that is being made. There is today a great conviction that humanity can improve its lot through action, be it political, social, or economic action; guilt feelings and similar personal problems can be relieved by psychiatry; drugs of one kind or another can alleviate most forms of pain, disease and depression; scientific development and technological advance can solve (if not today, then tomorrow) the various new problems which arise within our society. Such developments in western society have had a profound effect upon our state of mind. We tend now to look for help not from 'outside' our human society but rather from within that society. We no longer see ourselves and our predicament in the way in which people in the first century or even the nineteenth century of the Christian era did. The common sense of our western culture believes in a kind of universal salvation which is through our own human efforts. By national or international political or economic reorganization, we believe we can move toward peace and justice in the world and toward the elimination of poverty and disease. We possess and perpetrate a strong self-confidence.

Obviously, in this situation the Church can accommodate its message to the general consciousness within western society. It can hold and preach a message which is appreciated and understood in the terms of reference provided by the society itself. Salvation can be presented in terms of the results of the activity in which the Church ought to engage in God's name in one or another form of social or political activity. The Kingdom of God, a phrase much on the lips of Jesus, can be seen and presented only in this-worldly terms: the bringing of justice into human affairs. And, let us be honest, much of our activity as members of the Church has been based on this way of understanding; certainly, a lot of the work either initiated or sponsored by the World Council of Churches has tended to be of this kind.

There is a widespread fashion for reducing the proclamation of salvation to the kind of activism characteristic of political pressure groups. We are besieged by all kinds of demands to march against the bomb, to lobby against racism, to engage in protests of one kind or another. We are encouraged to 'do something about it'. Yet when the Church is thinking of, or actually engaging in this kind of activity, the question needs to be asked: Can we bring in the Kingdom of God and advance God's salvation by using the accepted tactics of our contemporaries and by reducing salvation to this-worldly terms? Against such understanding the writers of the New Testament, and thus the exalted Lord Christ, protest. They tell us that the human condition is fundamentally wrong and that, because of this, it was necessary for the Son of God to become a human being in order to be our Saviour.

It may well be asked: Why do you say these things about salvation, when apparently salvation is very popular and widely received in America? Do not the various studies show that over half the population claims to have made a decision for Christ, and to be born again? Certainly here we seem to have a problem. It is apparently the case that great numbers of Americans claim to enjoy God's salvation. My fear is that in many cases the salvation is not God's salvation in its fulness, since it is a 'salvation' which apparently does not get through the veneer of the outer casing of human lives and life-styles. So often 'salvation' appears to be a kind of synonym for God's approval of a particular form of individualistic understanding of Christianity coupled with certain political and social commitments, which tend to have a right-wing emphasis.

This is a very different phenomenon to the political and social activism of the World Council of Churches and of liberal-minded Christians in recent times. It is the other end of the swing of the pendulum. It is the individualistic search for a sense of being right with God; and this understanding of salvation can become a kind of approving seal upon the life and life-style of the one who makes a decision for Christ and is 'born-again'. So often the 'salvation' does not reach down to deal with the fundamental 'original sin' or 'gone-wrong-ness' or *hubris* which is there, endemic in the human nature which we all share. Thus it remains the case that, despite the many claims of salvation made in America, there is still need for the proclamation of a full salvation, which meets the deepest and most fundamental need of human beings in terms of their relationship with God, their membership of human society and their position in God's creation.

This means that the proclamation of salvation today must include the uncovering, or the laying bare, of the basic human predicament in the light of God's existence and revelation. Whether we call the basic human problem 'original sin' or 'gone-wrong-ness' it matters not. We can even go back to a word from classical Greek and talk about a massive, corporate *hubris,* a flaw in all human nature. There is a weakness, a fundamental gone-wrong-ness which is both in the individual and in society. Though we think we can see, in certain areas we are blind. Though we think we are healthy, in certain aspects of our existence we are chronically sick. The human race was created by God to enjoy spiritual union and communion with himself. Where this does not exist then there is a fundamental problem. For the human being is made to enjoy a relationship both with his Creator and with the creatures whom God has made. Only with right relationships with God, with human beings and with creation can a person find wholeness or salvation. We shall return to this theme of righteousness or justification below.

The message of salvation to the world must include the uncovering of the need which we all have for salvation. But even when this is done the Church can still make a mistake in the way in which it presents God's offer of salvation in Jesus Christ. This mistake can best be illustrated by considering two types of sentences. The first type we may call an 'if . . . then' statement. Here are several examples. Speaking to a child at table we say, 'If you eat your meat and potatoes, then you can have some ice cream'. To a child at school we say, 'If you pass your examinations, then we will buy you a bike'. To a young person starting work we say, 'If you do your work well then we will see that you get promotion'. Finally, we all are familiar with the politician who says, 'If you vote for me then I will do for you what you want me to do'.

This form of statement, with the understanding it encapsulates, is necessary for human society. But we make a major mistake if we present or understand the Gospel of God on this basis. In other words, if we make 'believe' or 'repent and believe' into a condition which we ourselves must fulfil by ourselves in order to get the reward of God's salvation, then we pervert the Gospel!

It is far better to think of the promise of salvation from God as it is described in the New Testament as being of the structure, 'because . . . therefore'. Here are a couple of examples. 'Because there is a free national health service, go into hospital for your operation'; and 'because the day is warm and the sand is clean go and bathe in the sea'. So the message of salvation is something like this: 'Because Jesus Christ died for your sins and rose for your acceptance with God, therefore you are saved'. And, 'Because God has provided salvation for you in Jesus Christ, therefore you are to believe and to receive this salvation'. And, 'Because God loves you and will love you, therefore you are to accept his love'.

You can see the difference between the 'if . . . then' and the 'because . . . therefore' approach. The first encourages us to think that we can do something to contribute to our salvation, while the second reminds us that salvation is, from beginning to end, the gift of God; and the gift is not earned but rather gratefully received and accepted. We do not ourselves offer to God our religion, our good works, our pious thoughts, and our good endeavors so that he will accept us. Rather we gratefully receive. We believe God and his promises concerning salvation, and then, out of sheer amazement and gratitude to him for his wonderful salvation, we live a life of love towards him and our neighbour. As the verse of the old hymn puts it,

> I would not work my soul to save
> For that my Lord has done.
> But I will work like any slave
> For love of God's dear Son.

As the apostle Paul said, 'By grace are you saved through faith, and that not of yourselves, it is the gift of God'.

As this matter of free salvation is so important let us look at it with the help of another illustration. Consider the common occurrence of two people — Joan and Joy for example — who have a quarrel which has left deep feelings of hurt in each of them. One day, to the surprise of Joy, Joan comes to her and, looking at her kindly and straight in the eyes, says, 'I forgive you'. The words are intended to be words of love and reconciliation. But, as Joy immediately recognized, as well as being sincere words of love reconciliation, they also contained a word of condemnation. You cannot forgive someone who is not guilty! It is not right to say to someone, 'I forgive you' unless you are sure that he or she is in the wrong and your relationship to him or her is in the right. But back to Joy. She took the words as including a word of condemnation and went away with a sense of deeper hurt and resentment, refusing to submit to the verdict of guilty. However, later on, as Joy thought about it, she came to the recognition that Joan was right to say 'I forgive you' because in fact she had been in the wrong. So she decided to go and see Joan and accept the offer of love and reconciliation, recognizing that in doing this she was accepting the verdict of guilty.

In Christian terms, a penitent heart is one that accepts the verdict of guilty while also accepting the word of love and peace and reconciliation. In Christ, God the Father has spoken to the world his word of 'I forgive you through the sacrificial death of my beloved Son' and 'I give you peace, reconciliation and redemption in Christ'. To accept this word is not easy for proud people because it means that you accept also the verdict of guilty on yourself. For only the person who is guilty has need of pardon and forgiveness! Nevertheless, the response you make to the Gospel of free salvation in and through Christ is not your own achievement, since Christ on your behalf has fully responded to the Father. As your representative and substitute he has offered and continues to offer the perfect response of faith, love, trust, and obedience to the Father in his life, death, resurrection, ascension and continuing intercession for us in heaven. What we could never do, he has done and is doing for us. So, when you accept the word of the Gospel, you accept not only God's gift to us in terms of the movement of Christ toward us from the Father; but, you also accept that gift in terms of the movement of Christ for us to the Father. Our penitence and faith is our being united to Christ in his great response to the Father for us.

This illustration of Joan and Joy allows us to make the distinction which was made by the early reformers in the sixteenth century between, on the one hand, legal repentance, and on the other, evangelical repentance. The reformers were insistent that much of the teaching on, and practice of, penitence in the late medieval Church proceeded on the wrong assumptions and was thereby distorted. To simplify the matter, the message so often heard in the late medieval Church was, 'Repent of your sins and *if you repent*, you will be forgiven'. This proceeded on the false assumption that God had somehow to be persuaded to be gracious and forgiving. The way that the reformers read the New Testament (and how they included it in the revision of the Liturgies) was like this. 'Christ has taken away your sins by his death on the Cross; he has conquered death, sin, Satan, and hell and now lives forever to be your Mediator and Saviour; therefore you are to repent'. In this way repentance is seen as a *response* to grace and not a *condition* of grace. The good news is that Christ has made the response to God which we ourselves are quite unable to make ourselves, and that therefore, we are called to accept this response of Christ — to respond to his response by believing the promises of God concerning him. So we see that forgiveness is logically prior to repentance. The word of forgiveness is included in the Gospel and only on this basis can we believe and repent. By grace are we saved through faith.

The grace of God is not some kind of heavenly fluid that flows through an invisible pipeline into your heart; nor is it a kind of heavenly injection into your soul given at baptism and in holy communion. Grace is the content of a relationship. Grace is the activity of God in relating to you, person to person, and restoring the broken relationship that there previously existed. Grace is the love and mercy of God in personal activity, searching for you, finding you, and restoring you to a life of fellowship and communion with himself. Grace is the continuing concern of God within this relationship to bless, guide, keep, and look after you in the fellowship of those who, like you, are in the process of receiving God's gift of salvation.

Of course, it takes two to make a relationship, and you may resist or reject that grace which is always searching for you, wanting to find you. The evangel, or the good news, is based upon, proceeds from, and is energized by the grace of God, Father, Son, and Holy Spirit. Without the grace of God there can be no Gospel. And because of the grace of God, therefore we are to believe, and therefore we are to receive, and therefore we are to love.

That salvation is by grace alone is clearly presented in the New Testament. Further, throughout her history, the Church has recognized and realized this truth. Sometimes she has neglected it, or sought to change it, with the result that the grace of God has been understood as the reward of human activity — the 'if . . . then' approach! This has caused much confusion; people have engaged in intense activity to seek to save their own souls and have found the activity useless. Such a person was Martin Luther, the German monk who was intensely religious as any monk could be. But all his intense activity, all his efforts to meet the conditions, as he saw them, of salvation led him only into deeper darkness of mind and depression. Then his mind was illuminated by the Holy Spirit and he saw the great truth that because Jesus Christ has died and rose again therefore in Christ — and in Christ alone — he is saved. In the next chapter we shall examine the doctrine that for Luther was *the* statement of the Gospel — justification by faith.

Proclamation

To preach justification or salvation today as a free gift of God can only be effective if our proclamation is the proclamation of the exalted Lord Jesus. Only if he, as the heavenly Prophet of God, by his Spirit takes our words so that they are effectively his words, will there be any movement of the human heart and will toward God. The problem is that the fundamental gone-wrongness or blindness or *hubris* of the human condition causes us to hear whatever is proclaimed to us according to our blindness and according to our gone-wrong-ness. Therefore, the proclamation of good news solely in the power of human rhetoric and persuasion cannot make any inroads into our fixed human condition. This is why the Church has always understood that only when preaching is in the might and power of the Holy Spirit can there be any success, in terms of causing illumination and faith to arise in the hearts of the hearers. In other words, only as the Church is in an effective fellowship with the Lord Jesus Christ, and he is able to use members of the Church to proclaim his prophetic word of good news in the power of his Spirit, can there be any success. It is he who illuminates the mind of the proclaimer, opens the heart of the receiver, persuading him that what he hears is truly good news, good news from God, which is able to make him a new creation before God.

To say that the Church is wholly dependent upon the activity of the exalted Lord and his Spirit does not excuse those who are preachers and teachers in the Church from careful preparation and exercise of their ministry. Paradoxically, the same exalted Lord who makes our words effective because they are, through the Spirit, his words, also calls upon, and expects, his messengers to be people who are thoroughly prepared in heart, mind and voice. Regrettably there is a lack today in some of the clergy of the sense of the high calling which is involved in being a preacher of the Gospel. This needs to change; but, even when the clergy do all within their power, as assisted by God, to prepare themselves for preaching and to engage in the act of preaching, they are still, as we have made clear, wholly dependent for their success, their genuine success, on the exercise and power of the exalted Lord Jesus.

The black preacher is reputed to have said: 'I reads myself full; I thinks myself clear; I prays myself hot; and then I do fire'. This procedure is not without merit! The point is that, unless preachers themselves are grasped by the very salvation they are proclaiming, and, unless preachers are in vital communion with the Lord of the Church, it is unlikely that their proclamation will bear fruit in terms of real and genuine salvation. If preachers have attractive personalities and are persuasive, they may have great success in terms of changing people's minds and behaviour patterns. But this is not what the Church, under her exalted Lord, exists to do. The Church exists to be the exemplar and the bearer of God's salvation to the world; and, in order to be and to do this, she needs to be a people who are dependent at all times upon the leading and the guidance of the Spirit of the exalted Lord Jesus. In his first letter to the Corinthian church Paul looked back on his initial experience in Corinth and wrote: 'When I came to you I was weak and trembled all over with fear, and my teaching and message were not delivered with skilful words of human wisdom, but with convincing proof of the power of God's Spirit'. That is how proclamation needs to take place — in dependence upon the exalted Lord and his Spirit. There is no other way for genuine success by the Church in the world.

The Church is not only the agent of evangelism, the bearer of the Good News; it is also a part of the message. The Gospel is directed toward real people in concrete situations, and people and situations differ. To be meaningful, the Good News has to be presented in different ways to different people. If the Good News is taken to the lonely and the alienated, then with the proclamation and explanation will go a continuing loving care and concern by the members. If the Gospel is taken to the poor and destitute then attempts will be made to relieve the poverty and change the structures which create poverty. Good News entails good works. They belong together. So evangelism cannot be separated from social action. The Church is inseparable in practice from the Gospel, for the Church witnesses by its attitude and actions as to the kind of people whom the Word and Spirit of the Lord create. Therefore, to preach and not to act, to proclaim and not to care, and to bear the Gospel and not to show practical concern is not truly to evangelize in God's mission.

We have seen how the Gospel is to be faithfully understood and proclaimed not only by keen lay Christians but also by the bishops, the parish priests and assistant curates. The larger one's office in the Church the greater should be one's commitment to the Gospel. Each bishop and priest should be known as a gospel-centered pastor, a person who delights to offer Christ to the Church and to the world. Likewise each deacon and deaconess should be known by their practical service of the Gospel. The exalted Lord Jesus sent his disciples into the world to preach the Gospel to everybody and to baptize those who believed in the name of the Father, Son, and Holy Spirit.

Baptism is a gospel sacrament. It is the sign of new life through Jesus Christ; it is the outward and visible means whereby a person is united to Christ and to the people of Christ. There is a richness of imagery in the New Testament to express the gift of God which is symbolized by baptism. Baptism is participation in Christ's death and resurrection (Rom. 6:13; Col. 2:12); a washing away of sin (1 Cor. 6:11); a new birth (John 3:5); an enlightenment by Christ (Eph. 5:14); a reclothing in Christ (Gal. 3:27); a renewal by the Spirit (Titus 3:5); and a liberation into a new humanity in which all divisions of sex, race, or social status are transcended (Gal. 3:27–8; 1 Cor. 12:13). The richness of the images points to the one reality of salvation.

Baptism is administered to those who believe and receive the Gospel and to the children of those who have responded to the Gospel. By its very nature it is unrepeatable. In the case of infants there is the further rite of confirmation, which is the completion of baptism. This provides the opportunity for the one baptized as an infant to make a public confession of faith and for the bishop, in God's name, to confirm the grace of God already given in baptism. In modern times we have recovered the understanding that baptism is intimately connected with the corporate life and worship of the people of God. Therefore now it is normally administered in a public service of worship. This practice rightly communicates the truth that baptism is into Christ and into the fellowship of the living church, while also giving members of the congregation an opportunity to renew their baptismal vows of commitment to Christ. Furthermore, in the Christian life, when we are tempted or tested we can look back to baptism and say,

'I have been baptised'. Baptism, as the sign and seal of God's free salvation in Christ, brings assurance of that same salvation.

A great problem for the Anglican Church has been, and remains, to have a realistic baptismal policy for each of its parishes. There has been too much indiscriminate baptism in the past, leading to a general devaluation of the sacrament and its effectual symbolism. We have been guided by the ancient principle of 'charitable supposition' and have perhaps forgotten that true charity includes being faithful to the good news of God and the life-style to which this points.

The Lord's Supper is the second gospel sacrament and occurs within the service that we now often call the Eucharist. Its celebration is the central act of the Sunday worship of the Church. We believe that through his Spirit Christ comes to us in the Eucharist to be the Preacher of the Word of God, to be the President of the meal, and to be the spiritual Food of that same meal. For the physical elements of bread and wine are the symbols of the spiritual food of Christ himself, the crucified Saviour, who is now the exalted Lord. In baptism we are incorporated into Christ, made members of his spiritual body; and in the Eucharist we are fed and sustained by Christ so that we can live in a way that adorns the Gospel which we exist to commend and proclaim. In the next chapter we shall return to the theme of eucharistic worship.

The truth is that when a congregation of the faithful is excited by the good news of salvation and is thrilled with the joy of forgiveness of sin and a right relationship with God, then all its worship is truly spiritual for it is gospel-centered. The ceremonial or actions of the service (e.g. breaking of the bread) the ritual or words of the liturgy (e.g. the 'Gloria') and even the dress of the clergy and ministers should be means of helping people to think of, and to come into touch with, the power of God.

Not a few Protestants are put off by some of the excessive ceremonial and ministerial dress that is found in some churches. This is because they suspect or fear that the symbolism or ceremonial points more to itself or to medievalism than to Christ and God's free grace. Thus it is extremely important that Anglicans are fully aware of the intention and meaning of all their activities, processions, postures, vestments and words within the church building. To take a simple example. The Gospel procession at the Eucharist may seem to an untrained eye as unnecessary or flamboyant activity! But, if it is perceived by the worshippers and can be explained by them as an outward sign, a visible way of emphasizing the priority of the Gospel (recorded in the gospels) in the Church and that the Gospel is the treasure of the Church, then an advance will have been made both in their religious experience and in their ability to communicate to others. In other words, Anglicans need to look critically at all their symbolism, ceremonial and ritual and make sure that it does have a reasonable, easily understood and explained reference to the Gospel and its effects on human lives. If the route from the symbol to the Reality is complicated then a question mark should be placed against its use in the Church.

There are some services used in a few churches which seem to go to the border lines of permissibility of symbolic communication. The service called 'Benediction' appears to be of this kind. The origins of this rite go back to the thirteenth century and more immediately to Roman Catholicism. Its function is to allow the worshippers to adore Christ through the (supposed) real and perpetual presence in the consecrated, reserved bread which is contained in the monstrance or ciborium. Built into this rite are several presuppositions; all have to be accepted for the worshipper to be able fully to participate. The result is that its validity and usefulness are made immediately suspect. For example, one is required to believe in a particular form of the real presence of Christ in the bread of the sacrament, that reservation of the sacrament for purposes other than the communion of the sick is valid, and that Christ can be the more readily encountered as the living Saviour in this rite than in a much simpler service of worship. But the strongest criticism is that it is not a gospel-centered rite; for, allowing for the best possible explanation of it as well as for an element of 'mystery', it does not have a sufficiently immediate reference to the Gospel of our Lord Jesus. Not everything that comes to us in the tradition of the Church is to be accepted and used; at times we have to drop certain rites and at other times revive, perhaps in new form, old forgotten rites.

Another area needs brief mention. If we are seeking to be wholly committed to the Gospel, then as Anglicans we must affirm our unity with those who, while not having (from our viewpoint) the catholic heritage and principles, nevertheless do sincerely and wholeheartedly preach the Gospel. We must affirm what is so prominent and important in these Protestant groups. We may say that they have the treasure of the Gospel without a right container in which to keep it. It may be a suitable container but it is not the one most appropriate for the treasure found within it.

If we are to say this, we must hasten to say that the Church which has the Gospel in the right container of genuine Catholicity is to be the Church which ceaselessly and lovingly proclaims the same Gospel. The Anglican Church should be the first to proclaim the good news to the world both in word and deed. Mission and evangelism, with the Gospel at their center, should be the priority in the relationship of the Church to the world around her. If the Gospel is precious to the people of God then they ought to make it precious for others. The jewel of the Gospel of God is not to be kept locked away; but, by its very nature it is to be shared with the whole world. When shared the jewel will be found to have an infinite capacity to reproduce itself where there is the fertile context of faith and repentance. The will of the exalted Lord is that we go into the world and preach the good news to all creation. At the present time, he has no other hands but our hands and no voice but our voices.

Yet, because we proclaim the Gospel as catholic-minded Christians, we do not proclaim the Gospel in a way which produces an individualistic faith. We proclaim Christ, and God's offer of forgiveness and new life in him in such a way that people enter and enjoy the fellowship and heritage of God's grace within the historical, continuing Church. We so proclaim the Gospel of Christ that we make it clear that those who respond to the Gospel recognize that Christian faith cannot be pursued in isolation, but is to be lived out within the fellowship of the local church, making full use of the sacraments, services and ministries there available. Far too much evangelism in this century has been isolated from commitment to Christ within his Church. It has not been made sufficiently clear that the Lord Jesus, who wishes to be the Lord of my life is already Lord of his Church into which by believing in him, he will place me. The new birth into the kingdom of God has societal implications; baptism is into Christ and into union with those who are already united to him; membership of the local church as a microcosm of the one Catholic Church is a necessary implication of genuine conversion to God; for the Christian life is normally to be developed and nurtured within the fellowship and worship of the local people of God.

But what of the relation of the historic Church to the so-called para-church organizations — e.g. Campus Crusade, Inter-Varsity, and Navigators? None of these is under the control of a Church

synod. They are independent organizations which have a tremendous impact on young people in their evangelism and enthusiasm for the good news concerning Jesus Christ. It cannot be
our duty to condemn, for the existence of such organizations is
often related to the lack of evangelism by the traditional churches.
Rather it is the duty of the Church to call the young people, who
have been or are in these organizations, to a fuller realization of
the nature of the Church on earth and to what we are calling its
Catholicity. Without losing their love for Jesus and the good news
concerning him, we need to guide them into the full enjoyment
of Catholicity so that we can gain from their joy in the Lord and
they can gain from our Catholic heritage and experience. In the
fullness of the life of the historical, continuing Church there is to
be found the potential and possibility of a richness that can never
be found in any other grouping or organization. It is that potential
which we need to make a reality for our young people. Let us
never forget that in God's design the Gospel was given to the
world to be the treasure of the visible, Catholic Church and to
permeate its life. Therefore we need to make room within the
Church for a fuller expression of the Gospel and a fuller utiliza-
tion of the gifts and enthusiasm of young people who have been
captured by the love of Christ. The Anglican Church needs to be
a living embodiment of the Gospel and, at the same time, the
bearer of the Gospel to the world.

4

By Faith Alone

Luther was the first to revive justification by faith as *the* way of explaining God's salvation in the Church; but, it quickly became the fundamental way in the Lutheran, Reformed and Anglican Churches to understand the central thrust of God's grace for persons in and through Jesus Christ. Together with other reformers, including our own Thomas Cranmer, Luther found this particular teaching in the writings of the apostle Paul, especially in the Letters to Galatia and Rome. The reason why the doctrine had such a powerful appeal was that the context in which St. Paul expounded it appeared to be much the same as the context provided by the late medieval Church in western Europe.

St. Paul expressed his teaching on righteousness/justification in response to those whom we usually call the Judaizers. They went into the churches of Galatia and said to the members: 'It is good that you believe in Jesus Christ as the Saviour of the world. But it is not good that you do not keep the basic requirements of the Law of Moses. All non-Jews who receive Jesus Christ as the Saviour and Lord need also to fulfill the basic rules of Judaism. This means that all males must be circumcised and that everyone should eat kosher food.' Here Christ was being presented as an incomplete Saviour. It was necessary, it was said, to add to his divine provision by fulfilling certain religious duties. St. Paul saw this with great clarity and protested vehemently. He affirmed and asserted that salvation is complete in Christ. There is nothing that human beings can do to add to the gift of God's salvation in Christ. Christians from a Gentile background are under no obligation whatsoever to keep the rules of Judaism.

Speaking for Christian Jews, St. Paul wrote: 'We are convinced that a human being needs to be accepted and declared righteous by God at the final judgement at the end of the present age.

Further, as Jews, we are convinced that such divine acceptance will never be achieved by fulfilling the laws, rules and ordinances of the Mosaic Covenant. Instead, we have come to see and know that acceptance by God occurs now — in anticipation of acceptance at the end of time — through the faith and faithfulness of our Saviour, Jesus Christ (who believed and obeyed the word of the Father when on earth, and who is now our Mediator in heaven). This gift of salvation provided in Christ we gratefully accept, gaining and experiencing thereby a right relationship with God our Father, through our Lord Jesus Christ' (paraphrase of Gal. 2:16). Therefore the only obligation which Gentile Christians have is to love God and to love other human beings. They are to love because God has first loved them, and because God places within them his Spirit to enable them to love as Christ loves the world.

St. Paul offered the same teaching in the Letter to Rome. The theme of the whole epistle is the righteousness of God. His opening statement is this:

> I am not ashamed of the Gospel, because it is the power of God for the salvation of everyone who believes: first to the Jew, then for the Gentile. For in the Gospel a righteousness from God is revealed, a righteousness that is by faith from first to last, just as it is written [in Habakkuk]: 'The righteous will live by faith' (NIV).

The good news is for the whole world and since it is the effective and effectual word of the Lord, proclaimed in the power of the Spirit, it achieves results. It brings salvation to sinners, Jew and Gentile alike, who receive and believe it. The clue to the saving power of the Gospel of God lies in the fact that God has acted in righteousness to make provision in Jesus Christ for our salvation. This means that God now reckons as righteous in his sight those who believe in the Lord Jesus. The 'righteousness of God' is a genitive of authorship meaning, 'the righteousness which goes forth from God' to place sinners in a right relationship to himself.

In the fifteenth and early sixteenth centuries it is fair to say that the message of salvation was certainly proclaimed as being based upon and centered in Jesus Christ. However, it was a message that also included the need for human beings to fulfil certain requirements in order to merit that salvation. The situation (to recall our previous chapter) was that of the 'if . . . then' approach.

If you do this and you do that, then you may hope to receive God's salvation. If you properly repent and do penance, and if you fulfil basic religious duties, then you may expect that God will give you his salvation, and you may hope that at the end of your life, when you face your Creator, he will justify you. Of course, there is nothing wrong with religious duties and with service within holy, mother Church. What is wrong is that something is made a condition of salvation when salvation is the gift of God. In fact, medieval Christianity had excessively developed, and given undue importance to, certain aspects of the Christian Faith and worship which in origin were good.

Here are three examples. First, the 'communion of the saints' is a basic doctrine of the Creed; but to have excessively developed a cult of the saints, so that the worship and service of Jesus Christ was thereby eclipsed, was to have gone in a wrong path of understanding and practice. And to bring the cult of the saints into the process of the granting of salvation by God to sinners was to have done too much with a good thing! Then, secondly, to think of Mary as the most wonderful woman who has ever lived is true Christian thinking. To call her *theotokos* (God-bearer), as the early Church did, is again very acceptable, for this title points to the deity of her Son. But, to have made her into a kind of go-between (mediatrix) so that a sinner has to go to her Son through her, is to add a dimension to the Gospel which is not even suggested in the New Testament. Thirdly, the common practice of granting indulgences, connected as it was with complicated views of the merit of the Virgin Mary, the saints and martyrs, and of the cancellation of the temporal punishment due because of sins, had gotten out of control. It was a religious racket to raise money to build great churches: but poor souls thought that it assisted in the salvation of their loved ones and themselves.

We could multiply the examples. The reformers of the sixteenth century saw all kinds of parallels between the emphases of the Judaizers, whom the apostle Paul had so strongly condemned, and the teaching of the bishops and priests of the Church of their day. They had been enabled by the divine Spirit to see very clearly that salvation is the gift of God and is received by faith. And they expressed that understanding in their teaching on justification by faith. This was not just any doctrine, it was *the* doctrine. It was not one article of faith among others; it was the *articulus stantis et cadentis ecclesiae* (the article of faith by which the Church stands or falls), and the statement of the essence of the Gospel.

As that which conveys the essence of the Gospel of God, the doctrine of justification by faith is an important theme in the formularies of the reformed Church of England of the sixteenth century (and therefore of the Anglican Communion). The Service of Holy Communion in *The Book of Common Prayer* stands as a testimony to the use of this doctrine in the renewal of the structure and contents of the medieval Mass. The duties of the bishop, priest and deacon, as portrayed in the *Ordinal,* reflect the influence of this doctrine. And the *Articles of Religion* (1563) contain four articles directly relating to the doctrine. Here are the first two:

XI. Of the Justification of Man

We are accounted righteous before God, only for the merit of our Lord and Saviour Jesus Christ by faith, and not for our own works or deservings: Wherefore, that we are jus-. tified by faith only is a most wholesome doctrine, and very full of comfort, as more largely is expressed in the Homily of Justification.

XII. Of Good Works

Albeit that Good Works, which are the fruit of faith, and follow after Justification, cannot put away our sins, and endure the severity of God's judgement; yet are they pleasing and acceptable to God in Christ, and do spring necessarily of a true and lively faith; insomuch that by them a lively faith may be as evidently known as a tree discerned by the fruit.

These two articles capture the 'Lutheran' understanding of salvation in which justification is seen as God putting the sinner in a right relationship with himself. God does this by his word of pardon and acceptance. This approach to justification, which is often called a forensic or declaratory approach, is different to the medieval view (which Roman Catholicism inherited). The latter is that 'to justify' is 'to make righteous'. As far as the Latin *justificare* is concerned the medieval Church was right; but it was wrong, and traditional Roman Catholicism has been wrong, to understand the Greek *dikaioo* used by St. Paul in Galatians and Ro-

mans to mean the same as *justificare.* The Greek verb has to do
with the declaration, rather than the process, of being in the right
with God. So in this instant, the Protestant insight, being based
on the Greek rather than the Latin New Testament, was correct.

The Homily on Justification (or, the Homily on Salvation) is the
third of the printed sermons in the *Book of Homilies,* provided
in the Elizabethan Church in order to be read in churches to ex-
plain the meaning of the Gospel. Archbishop Cranmer composed
the one to which Article XI refers. It insists that justification is the
act and gift of God.

> Because all men be sinners and offenders against God, and
> breakers of his law and commandments, therefore can no
> man by his own acts, works, and deeds, seem they never
> so good, be justified and made righteous before God; but
> every man of necessity is constrained to seek for another
> righteousness or justification, to be received at God's own
> hands, that is to say, the remission, pardon, and forgiveness
> of his sins and trespasses in such things as he hath offended.
> And this justification or righteousness, which we so receive
> by God's mercy and Christ's merits, embraced by faith, is
> taken, accepted, and allowed of God for our perfect and
> full justification.

Such statements effectively remove the support from under much
medieval 'meritorious' religion. Cranmer continued:

> It pleased our heavenly Father, of his infinite mercy, with-
> out any our desert or deserving, to prepare for us the most
> precious jewels of Christ's body and blood, whereby our
> ransom might be fully paid, the law fulfilled, and his justice
> fully satisfied. So that Christ is now the righteousness of all
> them that truly do believe in him. He for them paid their
> ransom by his death. He for them fulfilled the law in his
> life. So that now in him and by him every true Christian
> man may be called a fulfiller of the law; forasmuch as that
> which their infirmity lacketh Christ's justice hath supplied.

And, having made a special study of the early Fathers of the
Church, Cranmer proceeded to claim that they actually taught
that salvation is wholly the gift of God and that our good works
cannot contribute to our salvation. He held that the authentic and
primitive teaching of the Church had been corrupted in the medieval Church, with the result that a doctrine of salvation by works
was effectively recognized. So he protested:

> Justification is not the office of man, but of God. For man

cannot make himself righteous by his own works, neither in part, nor in the whole; for that were the greatest arrogancy and presumption of man that Antichrist could set up against God, to affirm that a man might by his own works take away and purge his own sins, and so justify himself. But justification is the office of God only; and is not a thing which we render unto him, but which we receive of him; not which we give to him, but which we take of him, by his free mercy, and by the only merits of his most dearly beloved Son, our only Redeemer, Saviour, and Justifier, Jesus Christ. So that the true understanding of this doctrine, We be justified freely by faith without works, or that we be justified by faith in Christ only, is not that this is our own act, to believe in Christ, or this our faith in Christ, which is within us, doth justify us and deserve our justification unto us; for that were to count ourselves to be justified by some act or virtue that is within ourselves. But the true understanding and meaning thereof is, that, although we hear God's word and believe it, although we have faith, hope, charity, repentance, dread, and fear of God within us, and do never so many good works thereunto, yet we must renounce the merit of all our said virtues of faith, hope, charity, and all our other virtues and good deeds, which we either have done, shall do, or can do, as things that be far too weak and insufficient and unperfect to deserve remission of our sins and our justification; and therefore we must trust only in God's mercy, and in that sacrifice which our High Priest and Saviour Christ Jesus, the Son of God, once offered for us upon the Cross.

The teaching of the reformed Church of England differed from the Roman Catholic Church on two points with respect to the Gospel as presented through justification by faith. First of all the Church of England declared that righteousness is imputed, or reckoned, to the believer because of the merit of Christ: this contrasted with the claim of the Roman Church that righteousness is infused into the soul. So, for the one, justification is forensic, and, for the other, it is moral. Then, while the Church of England fully commended good works as the fruit of genuine faith, it is not prepared in any circumstances to say that they are meritorious in terms of gaining salvation. In contrast, the Church of Rome actually taught the meritoriousness of good works in gaining ultimate salvation.

It is a long time since the sixteenth century, but the issue of whether justification is 'to declare righteous' or 'to make righteous' has not been finally solved. Major theological commissions

(Roman and Lutheran, and Roman and Anglican) are addressing themselves to the question in 1983–84 and perhaps the matter will be resolved. As it is, Catholicity appears to speak with two different voices. Is one right and the other wrong? Or are both right?

What follows is an attempt to make some preliminary observations concerning justification so that, not only is this doctrine rightly understood, but the Gospel itself is discovered in and through its exposition. Naturally, in the circumstances it is only a preliminary and a provisional statement. The method I shall adopt in presenting the doctrine here is not that of a straightforward exposition of justification by faith. Rather I shall present six separate theses each of which can stand alone as a theological assertion. However, as a group, they present a coherent approach to the possible place of the doctrine in theological thinking today. (See also my *Justification and Sanctification*, Crossway Books, 1983.)

Thesis 1. *That the teaching of the apostle Paul on righteousness and faith must be distinguished from the theological construct (which comes in various forms) and is usually called justification by faith.*

This is simply to say that biblical theology and church doctrine, though intimately related, are not identical. Put another way, the attempt to summarize Paul's teaching on righteousness and faith in Paul's own concepts and terms (which is what books on biblical theology seek to do) is not the same as the statement of the doctrine of justification by faith in a document produced by a theologian, a synod or a council (e.g. Articles XI–XIV of the Thirty-Nine Articles). What theologians attempt to do in creating church doctrine is to interpret the content of Scripture in order to meet contemporary needs and answer contemporary questions. In so doing, they often use concepts and illustrative images from both biblical and non-biblical sources (e.g. in the Nicene Creed we say 'of one *Being* with the Father' [non-biblical] and 'he *came down* from heaven' [biblical]). There is no doubt but that the doctrine of justification was expressed in the sixteenth century by Luther and others to meet their sense of need and to answer what they saw as vital questions concerning salvation.

What theologians usually claim is that justification by faith alone is a doctrine which is reflected or taught in the whole of the Bible and which is given particular clarity by Paul in his letters to Galatia and Rome. Thus when the doctrine is expressed it is stated in dependence on Pauline terminology. Yet there is no necessary reason why the doctrine need be stated in such heavy dependence on Pauline terminology. It is merely the case that to use Paul's concepts and imagery has appeared appropriate. (Whether Pauline concepts are still appropriate in western society is a question worth investigating; however in the sixteenth century this question was not raised.)

I make all these (what may seem to some obvious) points because many Christians have simply equated the particular teaching on justification they have received with the teaching of Paul. The actual relationship between what Paul taught in relation to his context (active Judaizers, the Mosaic covenant and Gentile believers) and what Protestants have taught in relation to their context (controversy with Roman Catholics and search for salvation) is not a simple equation. First, there are variations in Protestant expositions of Justification — e.g., between Lutheran and Reformed. Even if these are minor, they are significant in showing that the Pauline and Protestant doctrines are not strictly identical.

Secondly, the function of the Anglican doctrine of justification has been to isolate and to emphasize what is regarded as a pivotal and strategic understanding of the Gospel (= good news of the kingdom of God in and through Jesus Christ): yet because it has been stated in opposition to what was seen as an erroneous, mistaken and imperfect grasp of the Gospel in a large part of the Church, its expression is affected by this circumstance. This point is particularly obvious in the contents of the Thirty-Nine Articles:

XIII. Of Works before Justification

Works done before the grace of Christ, and the Inspiration of his Spirit, are not pleasant to God, forasmuch as they spring not of faith in Jesus Christ, neither do they make men meet to receive grace, or (as the School-authors say) deserve grace of congruity: yea rather, for that they are not done as God hath willed and commanded them to be done, we doubt not but they have the nature of sin.

XIV. Of Works of Supererogation

Voluntary Works besides, over, and above, God's Commandments, which they call Works of Supererogation, cannot be taught without arrogancy and impiety: for by them men do declare, that they do not only render unto God as much as they are bound to do, but that they do more for his sake, than of bounden duty is required: whereas Christ saith plainly, When Ye have done all that are commanded to you, say, We are unprofitable servants.

What is said here is meaningless outside the original context, wherein there was an intense debate about the value of doing good works before and after genuine conversion to God.

What applies at the theological, confessional level also applies at the level of popular preaching. It has been commonplace in evangelical preaching to assume that the people today who appear to want to earn their way to heaven are the equivalent of the Judaizers against whom Paul protested in the Letter to Galatia. It has been my experience, that the realization that the Anglican statement of justification should not be seen as a strict equivalent of Paul's teaching on righteousness and faith (in Romans and Galatians), has been a liberating factor in the development of theological understanding. It has opened up avenues of thought for people which were earlier closed.

Thesis 2. *That in the teaching of the New Testament it is the one indivisible grace of God which unites the believer to God in Christ for forgiveness and acceptance and which places him within the church, the people who walk by the Spirit and in love.*

Wherever you turn in the New Testament (as also in the Old Testament) it is a basic assumption and affirmation that those who love and worship God in truth are also to love their neighbors (howbeit imperfectly) as they love themselves. The branches joined to the vine have to bear fruit; the sheep are to follow the shepherd; believers in Christ are to walk in the Spirit: justification is by faith which works by love; those who love God are also to love the brethren; the elect are chosen in Christ in order to bring forth good works for God's glory; those who are baptized are to die to sin and live to righteousness; those who are forgiven are to forgive others; and disciples of Christ are to take up their cross and follow him.

A relationship with the Father through the Son by the Spirit and in faith is not seen in the New Testament as distinct from or possible apart from, a life of obedience and faithfulness in the community of faith, the church. The work of the Spirit (sent by the Father through the Son) in the hearts of sinners bringing them to regeneration and faith is not to be thought of as separated from the declaration of the Father that they are forgiven, justified and adopted for Christ's sake. The righteousness of Jesus Christ, the Mediator, which wholly satisfies the just demands of the Father is the very reality which the Spirit begins to create in the believer's heart. The one Spirit who gives to the sinner the gift of faith also indwells the sinner so that he may be called 'the temple of the Holy Spirit'. Or, looked at from the human standpoint, the faith by which the Christian is united to the Lord Jesus is inseparable from the commitment to God's mission in baptism, and to faithfulness to the Lord Jesus in life.

If you carefully read the two Letters in which Paul explains justification you find that what we may term the vertical relation with the Father through the Son and the horizontal relation in the Spirit and in the church flow into each other and are presented as inseparable (except, of course, in conceptual analysis).

Then, also, the word grace itself is used in the New Testament of all that God does for needy sinners. It can refer both to what God has provided objectively in Christ (see Rom. 3:23; 5:2,15,17) and what God does within his people (Rom. 5:21; 2 Cor. 8:1, 9:8; 2 Cor. 12:9). The grace of God is one. It is seen in the electing love of the Father, in the work of the Incarnate Son as Saviour and in the presence and work of the Holy Spirit within the Church.

Thus what God has united let us not divide asunder!

Thesis 3. *That while it may be helpful within Anglican teaching to divide the grace of God into justification and sanctification, it should always be remembered that God's grace is one and indivisible.*

Let us begin with an example of this theological division from the Westminster Confession of Faith (1647), now a Presbyterian Confession, but produced originally at Westminster Abbey for the Church of England!

Chapter XI. Of Justification

Section I. — Those whom God effectually calleth he also freely justifieth; not by infusing righteousness into them, but by pardoning their sins, and by accounting and accepting their persons as righteous: not for anything wrought in them, or done by them, but for Christ's sake alone: not by imputing faith itself, the act of believing, or any other evangelical obedience, to them as their righteousness, but by imputing the obedience and satisfaction of Christ unto them, they receiving and resting on him and his righteousness by faith: which faith they have not of themselves; it is the gift of God.

Section II. — Faith, thus receiving and resting on Christ and his righteousness, is the alone instrument of justification; yet it is not alone in the person justified, but is ever accompanied with all other saving graces, and is no dead faith, but worketh by love.

Chapter XIII. Of Sanctification

Section I. — They who are effectually called and regenerated, having a new heart and a new spirit created in them, are further sanctified really and personally, through the virtue of Christ's death and resurrection, by his Word and Spirit dwelling in them; the dominion of the whole body of sin is destroyed, and the several lusts thereof are more and more weakened and mortified, and they more and more quickened and strengthened in all saving graces, to the practice of true holiness, without which no man shall see the Lord.

Section II. — This sanctification is throughout in the whole man, yet imperfect in this life; there abide still some remnants of corruption in every part: whence ariseth a continual and irreconcilable war; the flesh lusting against the Spirit, and the Spirit against the flesh.

Section III. — In which war, although the remaining corruption for a time may much prevail, yet through the continual supply of strength from the sanctifying Spirit of Christ, the regenerate part doth overcome; and so the saints grow in grace, perfecting holiness in the fear of God.

Obviously this now common conceptual division used by preachers and theologians has advantages. It possesses clarity by distinguishing what God does in us and what God does for us, or what God states and declares concerning us outside the space-time continuum and what he achieves within us within the space-time continuum. Thus it easily fits into a scheme of systematic theology. Further, and this was important in the sixteenth century, it appeared to answer effectively the apparent Roman Catholic conflation or confusion of what God declares within his heavenly court and what God does within our earthly hearts.

But it also has certain disadvantages. One is that there is always a tendency to separate in practice and reality what is one activity of God — i.e. the conceptual division made for clarity becomes a real division and justification is emphasized as though it were possible to be declared righteous without being in the process of being made righteous. Consider the pastoral results when justification is described as though it can happen without the Spirit's work of making sinners holy. People are 'right with God' but not 'right with' their neighbors!

Then there is the problem that the biblical usage of 'sanctification' is more fluid than its use in Protestant doctrine. In the New Testament the people of God are not only called 'saints' (Rom. 1:7) but also described as already sanctified (e.g. Heb. 10: 10,14; Acts 20:2; 26:18; 1 Cor. 1:30, 6:11); here sanctification seems to have a function similar to that of justification, except that it is the holiness not righteousness of Christ in which God's people are clothed. Yet at other times sanctification is described as a process (e.g. 1 Thess. 5:23) and it is this usage which is taken up in Protestant doctrine. (Of course I am not saying that the first use of sanctification is denied or rejected by Protestants; I am merely remarking that the usage in systematic theology is not as fluid as in biblical theology).

It is important to recognize that, when this type of conceptual division of the grace of God is to be made, it must be recognized that we are dealing with two interrelated, interdependent and overlapping models. One model highlights the activity of God, the Spirit, within the sinner so that he becomes a believing sinner who is being made holy. By the inspiration of the Spirit the sinner believes on the Lord Jesus and this saving faith is accompanied by faithfulness to the Lord Jesus in daily life. From God's side this model may be called regeneration and from man's side conversion.

The second model highlights what God, the Father, as Judge declares. The picture is God's heavenly court where the sinner who believes in God, the Son, as Mediator is declared to be in the right and a member of God's covenant people. On the basis of his faith the sinner is declared to be righteous and to be a child of God. From God's side this model may be called the justification and acceptance of the sinner and from man's side saving faith.

This second model is dependent on the first (which highlights how faith in the Mediator arises); but also the first model is dependent on the second when it describes the continuance in faith and faithfulness of the believer. The knowledge which the believer has that he is forgiven, justified and accepted as a child of God is a strong, compelling incentive to follow continually the promptings of the Spirit, who now dwells within him.

Pastors and teachers in God's Church need to recognize the relation of these models to each other so that they will be careful always to unite what God has united — saving faith and faithfulness; imputed and imparted righteousness. And they also need to recognize something else.

In his *The Freedom of the Christian* (1520), which was widely read in Tudor of England, Luther presented two propositions which may be described as the two sides of the one coin.

1. A Christian is a perfectly free lord of all, subject to none.
2. A Christian is a perfectly dutiful servant of all, subject to all.

The first was his statement of the freedom enjoyed by those who are justified by faith: to them can come no harm for God, the only One who can harm them, has declared them to be in the right. Thus, being set free from selfish concern and care, those who are justified can give themselves wholly to the service of others. Because of the relationship in which the justified believer stands before God, he is free to serve and benefit others in all that he does, considering nothing except the need and advantage of his neighbor. True faith is active through love of the neighbor finding expression in joyful, cheerful and free service of others, and done without thought of hope of reward. When a believer is declared to be in the right before God there is nothing else he can want except to be like Christ who was the loving compassionate servant of all.

Even as justification by faith cannot be separated from membership of the covenant people, regeneration and personal holiness cannot be separated from the loving of the neighbor. A local church which thought and acted in this manner would have a tremendous impact in the neighborhood where God had placed it. Its members would be so busy serving their neighbors in whatever ways their neighbors needed help that they would find it natural to be involved in all the needs of the people — family, social, political, environmental, etc., — and would not have time to enjoy the luxury of asking whether the preaching of the gospel and social service belong together. That church would proclaim the gospel of Jesus inside the love of Jesus for the neighborhood.

Thesis 4. *That while justification by faith introduces an element of 'subjectivity' into Christian experience, this is not intended to become the basis for individualism or for the negation of the corporate life of the church and use of the sacraments.*

The experience of believing in the Lord Jesus and having the Spirit say to my spirit 'you are a child of God' is thrilling. It is wonderful to know God personally as Father and to be able to call him by the intimate name of 'Abba' (= my father). God's provision of salvation in Christ by the Spirit certainly fully meets the need felt by human beings for a personal relationship with God. Yet this personal relationship is intended by God to be enjoyed within the corporate life of the Church. The meaning of justification actually points to this divine intention. (Further, the exhilaration of the experience of salvation is not to become the basis of an individualistic salvation since assurance is related to God's promises and God's promises concern the covenant which is a corporate concept.)

Justification is God's declaration that a believer is in the right and now, through faith, a member of the covenant people. In God's lawcourt the law, which God himself gave to his people, is the covenant between himself and his people. For God to act righteously means to act according to that covenant. And justification in God's declaration that those who believe in Jesus Christ are within the covenant. It is a just declaration which is according to divine law; to declare a sinner to be just is only possible because to the sinner is reckoned or accounted the righteousness of Christ himself. Thus justification is not the means whereby it is possible for God to declare a believing sinner righteous; rather it is the declaration itself. In fact the declaration belongs properly to the Last Judgment but in the Gospel God declares his judgment now in anticipation of the last day.

If justification is God's declaration that a believer is in the covenant people then it follows (as Paul himself certainly taught) that justification and Baptism, justification and church membership and justification and Eucharist belong naturally together.

Baptism is the external sign and seal of membership of the covenant people given to a believer by God through his church. Thus we recall Luther's famous statement of Christian assurance: 'I have been baptised'. Membership of a local church (a community within the covenant) is both a natural sequel to baptism and a consequence of being indwelt by the one Spirit who indwells all believers and unites them. The modern notion that one can be justified by faith and not be committed as a member of a local church and participating in the Eucharist would have been anathema to the Reformers as it is also to Scripture. God's declaration that a believer is in the covenant people should be the basis for lively participation in the life of the covenant people in one's own locality.

It may also be stated that the doctrine of justification by faith has no definite bearing upon questions of high and low churchmanship and of ritual and ceremonial in worship. Those who know the worship of the Lutheran churches will be aware that in them a very high churchmanship and ornate form of worship goes happily hand in hand with a powerful affirmation of justification by faith. What the doctrine does is to require that all symbolism and ceremonial in worship point to the priority of the grace of God in human salvation.

Thesis 5. *That justification by faith and the pursuit of justice in the world are also intimately related.*

Already I have argued that membership of God's covenant community and commitment to holiness of life are inseparable from justification by faith. Here I want to claim that the community which is justified by faith and indwelt by the Spirit of God is a people who will desire to promote righteousness/justice in the world.

To be declared by the Father to be in the right, to have Christ's righteousness reckoned by the Father to us as if it were our own, is to be declared to be involved in God's mission in the world. Baptism also may be understood as incorporation into the people who join God in his mission in and to the world. A part of this total mission is to reveal in the life of the churches and in Christian involvement in local affairs what the righteousness of God is and demands. The people of God, who are being made righteous because they have been declared righteous, are to work in society in order to realize, at least in part, God's righteous/just standards. The Church of God is truly blessed when it longs or hungers and thirsts after God's justice being known now in this world before its fullness in the age to come.

Those who are justified by faith will certainly want to proclaim the Gospel of the Kingdom to the world; but since those who are justified are those in whom the fruit of the Spirit is growing, the love of God planted in their hearts will make them long for justice in human affairs. God's righteousness which is also the righteousness of Christ reaches beyond the creation of a new humanity or new covenant people to the creation of a new existence, a new age of the Kingdom of God. In the age to come God's righteousness will be wholly revealed and wholly known: now it is known in part and hoped for. But the people of God who are declared righteous will work to bring signs of that future justice in their own time. They will work to gain justice for those who may be deprived of it — the poor, aged, infirm, deprived, refugees, minority groups, etc. They will preach the Gospel of the Kingdom *inside* the love of the neighbor which ensures concern for the total situation of those who hear the Gospel.

To those who are declared righteous the existence of injustice and unrighteousness anywhere in God's world is unendurable and unacceptable. They have to do something about it. The justified must work for justice. They have no alternative.

The connection between justification by faith and bringing righteousness/justice into human affairs becomes even more obvious when the meaning of righteousness/justice in the Old Testament (on which the New Testament builds) is remembered. 'Righteousness in the Old Testament is the fulfilment of the demands of a relationship, whether that relationship be with men or with God. Each man is set within a multitude of relationships: king with people, judge with complainants, priest with worshippers, common man with family . . . community with resident alien and poor, all with God. And each of these relationships brings with it specific demands, the fulfilment of which constitutes righteousness. . . . When God or man fulfils the conditions imposed upon him by a relationship, he is, in Old Testament terms, righteous' (*Interp. Dict. of Bible*, 4, p. 80).

Thus it is the case that the people of the covenant (the family of God and body of Christ) are set in relationships not only within the covenant but also with the world around. In all these relationships as well as with God they seek for justice: in the case of God they are declared righteous for the sake of Christ but in all other relationships they are to work for justice as they are empowered by the Holy Spirit, who is the Spirit of righteousness and justice.

So, far from being an individualistic and anti-social doctrine, justification by faith preserves personal religion while imposing strong community and social demands. There is in the Church today a great concern for justice in God's world and with this concern there often too appears to go a supposition that justification by faith is an irrelevancy. In other parts of the Church there appears to be no connection made between justification by faith and justice in the world. What I am affirming is that justification by faith, the Church of God and the concern of the Church for justice in God's world should not be separated in the practice of Christianity in the world today.

It is not, I think, without significance that (at least in the sixteenth and seventeenth centuries) those who strongly affirmed the truth of justification by faith, also strongly affirmed the need for social and civil righteousness. This point holds even though we may think that the view of justice held by the Protestants in those days was not so enlightened as our view today. Further, as was noted in discussing thesis 3, Luther's statement of Christian freedom has within it the potential for the development of concern for justice in society.

Thesis 6. *That Anglican, Protestant and Roman Catholic theologians should make every effort to come to a common mind on what is the biblical teaching on justification and what are its implications for the Church today.*

It is my view that if Protestants can agree that there are legitimate and necessary connections between justification and holiness of life, justification and committed church membership and justification and justice for society, then they can talk humbly and confidently with Roman Catholics with whom they have disagreed for so long on these matters.

Traditionally Roman Catholics have accused Anglicans and Protestants of making Justification into a legal fiction — something declared in God's heavenly court which has no necessary simultaneous expression here below in real life situations. This accusation is not made so often today and loses its force if it is recognized that justification is the declaration that a believer is already in the covenant, a member of the family of God, and thus committed to holiness and church life.

*   *   *

Perhaps we are moving into an era when Western society needs to hear the Gospel in terms of justification by faith, and when the Church will be able to hold this dynamic teaching in the context of a genuine Catholicity. Certainly God's justifying righteousness and participation in Catholicity belong together.

PART 2

Catholicity

5

The Anglican Experience

Do you mind the Roman Catholic Church calling itself 'the Catholic Church', deliberately leaving out the adjective 'Roman'? I must confess that I do and so I normally refer to that important Church as 'the Roman Catholic Church'. This reference does not proceed from bigotry but out of a desire to recognize that Catholicity is not confined to that community.

The Catholic Church

First, let us do a brief word study. *Ekklesia* was the word used in the city-states of ancient Greece to describe the assembly of all the citizens. A democracy functioned in this assembly as the citizens voted on major issues such as whether to make war or a treaty of peace with another state. When the Hebrew Bible was translated from Hebrew into Greek, just before the time of Christ, the Jewish translators used *ekklesia* for the *kahal* — the congregation or the assembly of Israel. In using *ekklesia* they gave it a new reference — the call of the Lord. *Ekklesia* became the body of people, the assembly of Israel, who had been summoned from their homes to meet with God and to do his bidding (see Psalm 26:12; 68:26; Numb. 1:18; Judg. 20:2). It was God's elect people coming to meet and hear him.

The apostles used *ekklesia* to describe the community of the disciples of Jesus Christ. On a few occasions *ekklesia* refers to the total number of Christians on earth (e.g. 1 Cor. 12:28; Eph. 5:25). More often it refers to a local assembly or congregation of Christians (1 Cor. 11:18; 14:19,23; Gal. 1:2). By far the commonest description in the New Testament is, surprisingly, not the '*ekklesia* of Christ' but the '*ekklesia* of God' (1 Cor 1:2; 2 Cor. 1:1; 1 Thess. 2:14; 1 Tim. 3:5,15). So the local *ekklesia* is the assembly of people who have been called out of the world to meet with God. We usually translate *ekklesia* as 'church', but this is slightly confusing since the word church (derived from *kyria-kon* — a thing belonging to the Lord) can also refer to the actual building in which worship occurs.

Secondly, the word 'catholic' (from the Greek *katholikos*). This is not found in the New Testament and first occurs in Christian literature in the early second century in a Letter of St. Ignatius of Antioch to the church in Smyrna. Ignatius wrote: 'Where the bishop is to be seen, there let all his people be; just as wherever Jesus Christ is present, we have the *catholic* Church' (Sec. 8). So the primary sense of Catholicity is the presence of the living Christ who is recognized, worshipped and obeyed as Lord. As used of the Church it came to mean the world-wide Church in contrast to the local congregation and to refer to the faith confessed by that world-wide Church. Thus 'catholic' implied both universality and orthodoxy. So where the Church in one area or country knew itself to be one in faith with the Church in other lands and saw itself as a part of that whole Church, then it used the adjective 'catholic' of itself. On this view the Church in one area is a microcosm of the whole Church of God, militant here on earth and triumphant in heaven.

Fundamental to the twin ideas of universality and orthodoxy is the conviction that Jesus Christ is the Lord of, and Life-Giver to, the Church across space and through time. So to be catholic-minded is to say: 'It is my privilege and joy to belong to Jesus Christ, to be called by God into the assembly of believers. It is also my privilege to belong through that assembly of believers to the whole Church, which has existed under his rule through the centuries in many geographical areas'. To receive and accept the Church as it has existed, and as it has believed, taught, confessed and worshipped, is the beginnings of true Catholicity. Though only a part of the whole Church, the Anglican Communion rejoices in being a part and in sharing the one Lord, faith, baptism and hope of the total number of the faithful on earth. It also salutes the rest of the catholic Church and looks forward to growth toward greater understanding and cooperation. Further, in 'the communion of saints', it looks beyond space and time to the Church triumphant in heaven: 'With angels and archangels and all the company of heaven we laud and magnify thy holy name'.

In the Apostles' Creed we say: 'I believe in the Holy Spirit, the holy Catholic Church, the communion of the saints, the remission of sins, the resurrection of the body and the life everlasting'. This Creed was originally used in Italy by believers who were being baptized; only later did it become the Creed used daily in worship. The original Latin words make clear that while a Christian is to *believe in* the Holy Spirit (*credo in Spiritum sanctum*), he is to *believe* the Church (*credo ecclesiam*). To *believe in* God is to have saving faith in God. To *believe* the Church is to be a member of the Church, to accept that it came into being by God's will, and that it is a people in whom the Holy Spirit dwells. Therefore it is Catholic and Holy.

Roots in History

Biblical scholars point out that there are some ninety or so images of the Church of God in the New Testament. Some of these highlight the dynamic fellowship and sharing in which Christians are to engage — e.g. 'the body of Christ' (1 Cor. 12). Others, that of the 'people of God' (1 Pet. 2:9–10) for example, point to the historical continuity of the Church through history by recalling the historical pilgrimage and experience of the Israelites. To be catholic-minded is not to look back over the experience of the people of God with nostalgia or sentimentality. Rather, it is to look back, while also looking up, for the Church which has a historical, continuing existence also has a heavenly Lord. It was he who said that the power of death would not triumph over the Church which he would build (Matt 16:18). To look back, while also looking up, allows us to see the Church both as it is governed and sustained by the exalted Lord, and also as it is judged by him.

So we affirm the whole history and experience of the Church in the light of Jesus Christ. This is because it has been and remains, with all its strengths and weaknesses, successes and failures, the actual Church of God; it was set in motion by the Lord, and sustained, guided, chastised and judged by him. And always it has borne his name, sometimes faithfully and often unfaithfully, and so always in need of heavenly pardon. We cannot escape our relation to the Church through space and time. We cannot avoid roots in history — just as the plant cannot exist without roots which draw food from the soil and as I, and you, cannot exist without my, and your, family tree (biologically speaking).

Let us be clear. We cannot separate what we may call the inner nature or essence of the Church from either its varying historical form or its many functions in the world. In theoretical thinking such a conceptual division is possible and helpful; but, in actual experience, the form and actual historical presence of the Church are inseparable from its true nature as the church of God. We cannot separate the essence of the Church from its historical reality as we can distill salt from salty water; and we cannot practically distinguish its true nature from its visible, empirical existence as we may remove the husk from the kernel of corn. Its divine and human aspects (suggested by such an image as 'temple of the Holy Spirit', 1 Cor 3:16) are inextricably linked together, just as in Jesus of Nazareth, who is perfectly God and perfectly human. The humanity of the Son of God was and is a perfect humanity: the humanity of the Church in which the Spirit dwells is an imperfect humanity. It is this imperfection which is the source of the heresies, divisions, sins of omission and commission, and countless other aberrations in the life of the Church.

But let us not forget that it was the catholic Church, with its imperfections, that gave recognition to what we now call the canon of the New Testament. Over a long period there were circulated among the churches what we now recognize as the books of the New Testament, together with other books not in the collection. It was the Church which made the final selection of what went into the Canon. To say this is not to claim that the Church is above the Bible! Rather it is to say that, while the Church was created by the Gospel, the books in which the Gospel is presented and explained were collected and recognized as true bearers of the Gospel (or records of divine revelation) by the historical, continuing, catholic Church of the second to the fourth centuries. Parallel developments in the Church in this same general period of time included the general recognition of the threefold ordained ministry of bishop, presbyter (= priest) and deacon, the centrality of the Eucharist as the main act of worship on the Lord's Day, the creation of creeds (e.g. the Apostles' and Nicene) and the recognition of apostolic tradition (having reference to both the succession of sound teaching and to the historical, personal succession of bishops).

Now I realize that this appeal to the importance of the historical experience and wisdom of the Church does not necessarily have an immediate impact on people today. There are loud cries for modernity and relevance: and, of course, these are not wholly to be denied. The fact is that our technologically-based society, in which gadgets go out of date overnight, is a culture which does not easily breed confidence in the achievements of an earlier generation, especially an ancient generation in the pre-scientific world. But, let us not overlook the fact that worship, piety, spirituality, theology and philosophy in the Church are not the types or kinds of human achievement that quickly go out of date. We must resist the temptation to be led away from our roots in history. Christianity is, after all, a historical Faith in that God has revealed himself not in philosophical principles but to people and in events within history. The eternal Son of God actually became man and actually had a personal history within our space and time. Therefore a Christian must not undervalue the way in which God has led his people through the years.

On the other hand, we must not claim too much from history. This is possibly a fault of traditional Roman Catholicism. Here the tendency is to see as the will of God the results of all historical development, be that development the position of the Bishop of Rome in Christendom as the Vicar of Christ and apostolic succes-sor of St. Peter as head of the order of bishops, or the special dogma concerning Mary, mother of our Lord (i.e. the dogmas of the Immaculate Conception and of the Bodily Assumption). No human society, even when it has the promise of being guided by the exalted Lord and his Spirit, can ever be infallible on this earth in this imperfect age. The humanity of the Church is a fallen hu-manity. Only God, strictly speaking, is infallible; only he is free from error in every thing he thinks, says and does. The Church composed of human beings in the way of salvation can never be as God; part of their human predicament is their gone-wrong-ness and this means that they are prone, even in sincerity, to deceive themselves and believe themselves to be right, even when they are wrong.

Therefore, it is advisable to use another word than infallible to describe the historical experience of the Church. Perhaps the word that conveys the general idea that Christ is Lord of his Church, and will not allow it to stray too far from the way in which he wants it to walk, is *indefectibility,* meaning not subject to major or sustained error. Other possibilities are 'indestructibil-ity' and 'imperishability', but indefectibility seems the better word to convey the idea that the Church remains basically in the truth in spite of its constant errors, heresies and false paths and ways. Over the years the Church has been faithful to her Trinitarian Faith (expressed in the Nicene Creed and Liturgy). Perhaps it is true to say that the way in which the western Church has most

erred is not by denying the central truths but by excessive development of certain teaching, especially (as we noted) concerning
the Bishop of Rome and the Blessed Virgin Mary, and of certain
rites, excessive veneration of Mary and the saints, for example.
Regrettably such excessive, exaggerated or imbalanced development (which could be called 'corruption') has the effect of cloud-
ing the truth of the Gospel of free salvation in Jesus Christ.

Catholic and Reformed

To affirm Catholicity means that we cannot be too selective in
the way in which we look back to evaluate the long experience
of the Church of God. A fault of most Protestant denominations
has been, and remains, that of working from a limited perspec-
tive, choosing this and rejecting that. We are to accept the broad
and sustained themes of Catholicity and to reject deviant and exaggerated developments and expressions.

When the reformers of the Church of England in the mid-
sixteenth century attempted 'to wash the dirty face' of the national
Church, they recognized and made a .part of the Church's reformed existence the following catholic emphases.

1. The priority and authority of the Scriptures as the source of
   our knowledge of God.
2. The doctrinal guidance of the Catholic Creeds — Apostles',
   Nicene and Athanasian (Quicunque Vult).
3. The truth that salvation is, in the final analysis, the gift of God
   and by grace alone.
4. The use of Liturgy, which is faithful to Scripture and embodies the experience of the Church in worship over the centuries.
5. The historic episcopate or the order of bishops as a sign of
   the unity of the one Church of God. Unlike Scottish and
   Continental reformers, who ditched episcopacy because they
   saw it as too involved in the corruption which they knew
   must be removed, the English reformers insisted on the re-
   tention of the historic order of bishops.
6. The threefold ordained ministry of bishop, presbyter (= priest)
   and deacon, as that ministry which God has led the Church
   to adopt from primitive times.
7. The two Gospel sacraments of Holy Baptism and Holy Communion as instituted by Christ for regular use in the Church.

8. The unity of the ministry of the Word and Sacrament in the service of Holy Communion.
9. The need for regular preaching and teaching from the Scriptures.
10. The recognition that the visible unity of the Church on earth is God's will.
11. The need for a regularly reviewed canon law and moral theology.
12. The priesthood of the whole Church as a worshipping and praying society.

The approach, which these emphases reflect, was called 'reformed catholicity'.

Because of the particular historical circumstances of the sixteenth century, the affirmation of reformed Catholicity meant the denial of the excessive claims of the Papacy and the repudiation of certain medieval doctrines — in particular, the medieval dogma of transubstantiation (that the whole bread becomes the true body of Christ and that the whole wine becomes the true blood of Christ). A careful study of the formularies of the Church of England will reveal how reformed Catholicity was expressed. The Thirty-Nine Articles of Religion state the faithfulness of the Church of England to Scripture and true Catholic tradition. The Book of Homilies illustrates in sermon form what reformed Catholicity means for people in the pews. *The Book of Common Prayer* provides services of worship which teach Scriptural doctrines through revised, traditional forms, and the Ordinal contains services for the consecration of a bishop, the ordination of a priest and the making of a deacon.

The Catholicity claimed by the Church of England (and therefore by the Anglican Communion) is rightly called a 'reformed Catholicity' in contrast to what may be called a late medieval corrupted Catholicity. It was reformed because its roots were deep in the Scriptures and the experience of the Church of the first five centuries. By 1559, the year of the Elizabeth Settlement, the Church of England was not a new Church (whose origins lay in the legislation of Henry VIII), but a renewed, revitalized, reformed Church, wholly committed to its position in the continuing historical existence of the Church of God in England (whose origins reached back to the ancient Celtic Church). Of course, it was not a perfect Church; it was, however, moving in the right direction.

Because the Church of England was attempting to be gospel-centered, it is also appropriate to call the Church of England a Protestant Church (and so to call the American Church the 'Protestant Episcopal Church'). This is because the meaning of 'Protestant' in England from 1530 until at least 1640 included the designation of catholic. 'Protestant' comes from the 'Protestation' drawn up by a minority at the Second Diet of Spires (1529) in Germany. Part of this statement is as follows: 'We are determined by God's grace and aid to abide by God's Word alone, the Holy Gospel contained in the biblical books of the Old and New Testaments. This Word alone should be preached, and nothing that is contrary to it. It is the only Truth. It is the sure rule of all Christian doctrine and conduct. It can never fail us or deceive us. Whosoever builds and abides on this foundation shall stand against all the gates of hell, while all merely human additions and vanities set up against it must fall before the presence of God.' The *Protestation* (from to protest = to make a solemn declaration) is a solemn declaration of faithfulness to the Gospel, written in Scripture, as the final court of appeal in the Church of God. Only in a secondary sense did Protestant mean a protest against the errors supported and encouraged by the Papacy. In essence, Protestantism is an appeal to the Lord Jesus, to Scripture, and to the early, patristic Church, against all later degeneration, error and apostasy. In this sense the Anglican Communion must be Protestant. Regrettably, however, the negative meaning of Protestant appears to have triumphed in the common understanding, and so today the word 'Protestant' is seen as one who is against Roman Catholicism. Therefore, if as Anglicans we are going to use the word 'Protestant', let us use it as meaning 'committed to genuine Catholicity'.

In Anglicanism we have long held that to maintain a genuine Catholicity (and to be truly Protestant) we need to be guided by Scripture, tradition and reason (in that order). The historical, continuing Church is the guardian and translator of the sacred Scriptures, but since the latter are the record of God's revelation to mankind, they stand always as the judge and guide of the Church as she is led by the Spirit of her exalted Lord. So the Bible must be the final authority in matters of faith and conduct. Yet this holy book has to be interpreted, understood and used in the life of the Church. It is here that tradition helps for it brings to us the experience of the catholic Church over the centuries (and before and after the Reformation). Tradition is that wealth of experience contained in written and unwritten sources which are passed on from generation to generation. It includes the way in which the Bible has been understood and put into practice in all kinds of activity and in various written forms (e.g. creeds, liturgies, canon law, theology and devotional books).

The place of reason (as it is illuminated by the Holy Spirit) is to look at Scripture in the light of the ethos and content of the catholic tradition and with questions arising from a particular society and culture. Thus decisions of a theological, moral, spiritual, political and economic nature are made on this solid basis. The human mind and conscience is fully informed before action is taken.

The stream of tradition which is ours to receive is deeper and longer than that which was received by the reformers of the Church of England in the sixteenth century. We have the experience of a divided Christendom, and its various minor streams, to receive and examine. Thus, for example, we are made aware of such matters as the possibilities of freedom in worship, of the ministry of the whole laity of God, of the world mission of the Church, and of our social calling as Christians in the modern world. Further, the questions raised by our increasingly technologically-based society become more difficult, not only in the field of medicine but in most areas of human development and growth.

Facing our complex society with Christian eyes, it would be wrong to abandon the classic approach of looking to Scripture with the help of tradition in the light of reason. Such a procedure preserves us from excessive individualism and where it does not easily lead to an answer to a modern, urgent question, at least it sets a good context for a Christian approach to an answer. Sometimes it will be painful to make decisions and sometimes wrong answers will be found. An example of a problematic question is that of whether a woman should be free to be ordained priest and consecrated bishop. Here we have the situation of tradition speaking with a strong voice in the negative, and reason finding it difficult to find any solid reasons why a woman should not be a candidate for, or called to, such an office in the Church of God. Regrettably the Anglican Communion has not moved as one body in answering this question and thus, when we do achieve a consensus of what is the will of Christ, there will be need for reconciliation within the Church.

Because Anglicanism has followed the appeal to Scripture, tradition and reason, it has been committed also to the creative concept and practice of comprehensiveness. Rightly understood, comprehensiveness is not the acceptance of a ragbag of assorted views and practices. It is not the expression of the principle that theological relativism is inescapable or even a good thing — i.e. that each of us does their own thing because there is not one truth to which we all ought to be committed.

Comprehensiveness is unity in fundamentals with the recognition in secondary matters, especially rites and ceremonies, that there can be differences of opinion and interpretation. The fundamentals are those found in the catholic Creeds and those presupposed in the Liturgy. So people belonging to different schools of Anglican interpretation (e.g. Evangelical, Anglo-Catholic and Latitudinarian) have been agreed on basics and in the use of a common form of Liturgy. Low Church, High Church and Broad Church have existed alongside each other and often overlapped with each other. (See Appendix 1.)

Recently the honored principle of comprehensiveness has been severely theatened by the appearance of radical theologians who provide interpretations of Christianity totally out of harmony with earlier interpretations. The old Latitudinarians did not deny the fundamentals of Trinitarian Faith, but claimed the right to explore areas around the center or essence of that Faith, and also to study the implications of the Faith with respect to new forms of learning. With the modern 'liberals' (better 'radicals') we have the arrival of people who deny the fundamentals. Not only is there the enthusiastic rejection by them of the doctrine of the Holy Trinity and the true deity of our Lord, but there is also a rejection of the authority of the primary and unique witness to Jesus provided in the gospels and epistles of the New Testament. They propose what they think are not merely novel but actually superior ways of thinking of Jesus and his place in history and in the search for salvation. They complain that recent liturgical revision within the Anglican Communion has not taken account of 'modern' theology. We reply that the Liturgy is based on a doctrinal foundation that has been tested and tried over the centuries and is as applicable today as it was yesterday.

Let us be frank. There is no room within the true comprehensiveness of Anglicanism for people to act as our theologians, teachers and priests who continue to deny the fundamentals of the Faith as they have been received, believed, taught and confessed over the centuries. There can be and should be new ways of expressing old truths; but this is a very different activity to the actual denial of old truths and the proposing of new ones. The Incarnation is in no sense a myth and if we lose our belief that the eternal Son of God genuinely assumed our human nature and flesh, then we also lose the authentic Christian Faith. And if God incarnate disappears, so also does true salvation. We need our bishops to lead us in joyfull commitment to the genuine Faith. Our liturgies, old and new, do preserve and commend the genuine article! For this we thank God.

One beneficial result of the arrival of the radicals has been the closer cooperation of members of the Evangelical and Anglo-Catholic schools of thought. They (together with others of 'no school') have united in defence of the received fundamentals which are derived from divine Revelation. This gives some impetus to the adoption of the vision that Anglicanism becomes simultaneously wholly committed to the Evangel and to Catholicity. It also provides some hope that our radical friends will eventually submit to the authentic Faith and not use the Church as the society and place in which to offer their latest and 'brightest' thoughts. We do not want to drive them from worship and sharing in the life of the people of God. We want them to submit with us to the Lord Jesus and to serve him together. But, until they return to belief in the fundamentals, we cannot see how they can be allowed to preach in our pulpits and to lecture to ordinands in our seminaries. (See Appendix 2.)

True Catholicity or reformed Catholicity requires genuine unity without uniformity. Comprehensiveness refers to that unity functioning without uniformity. Since most Anglican Churches now have a variety of liturgies, we are already gaining experience in terms of worship of what unity without uniformity can mean. When we become wholly evangelical and wholly catholic we shall understand it even better!

6

Pertinent Examples

Catholicity is a broad and deep theme. To convey what it means in practice, three examples are here provided. It will be recognized that Catholicity is not merely the possession of certain structures and activities; it is also a mood, an ethos, a spirit.

Bishops

A careful reading of the New Testament reveals that it does not describe or prescribe a single pattern of ordained ministry in the apostolic churches. It does not give us a blueprint or authoritative norm of forms of ordained ministry. But, as the Church was led through history by the exalted Lord through his Spirit, there gradually developed a settled and universal (catholic) pattern of ordained ministry. In the second and third centuries a threefold pattern developed of bishop, presbyter (= priest) and deacon. But the function of each order of ministry did not remain constant as time went by.

If we were to go back and visit a typical parish in the eastern Mediterranean world of the third or fourth centuries we would find, not a priest in charge (as in most Anglican parishes today) but rather a bishop. In that local congregation there would be the bishop, several presbyters and several deacons (and even further male ministers called subdeacons, acolytes, and readers). We would also find women engaging in various ministries as 'widows, virgins, and deaconesses', entrusted with duties of intercessory prayer, pastoral guidance and social work. Thus in the earliest days the bishop was the leader and pastor of a single community in which he preached and taught the Word of God, and presided at the Sunday Eucharist. He was assisted by a group of presbyters and deacons. But, as time progressed, there were attached to that single congregation other congregations over which the bishop assumed pastoral oversight. So there evolved what we now call dioceses, each one ruled by a bishop. This meant that each local congregation came to have a presbyter as its pastor and thus the senior local priest assumed a similar function to that of the bishop in former days. (I use 'presbyter' and 'priest' interchangeably since priest in Anglican usage is derived via medieval Latin from the Greek *presbyteros*.)

In the early centuries, and since that time, the bishop has been seen as the sign (but not the guarantee) of the unity of the one Church of God through space and time. He has been viewed as a living symbol and personal sign of the unity of the Church. This is why when a priest is consecrated bishop, other bishops, representing the one Church, set him apart to fulfil the calling in this order and office of ordained ministry. The presiding bishop says to the bishop-elect:

> A bishop is called to lead in serving and caring for the people of God and to work with them in the oversight of the Church. As a chief pastor he shares with his fellow bishops a special responsibility to maintain and further the unity of the Church, to uphold its discipline, and to guard its faith. He is to promote its mission throughout the world. It is his duty to watch over and pray for all those committed to his charge, and to teach and govern them after the example of the Apostles, speaking in the name of God and interpreting the gospel of Christ. He is to know his people and be known by them. He is to ordain and to send new ministers, guiding those who serve with him and enabling them to fulfil their ministry. He is to baptise and confirm, to preside at the Holy Communion, and to lead the offering of prayer and praise. He is to be merciful, but with firmness, and to minister discipline, but with mercy. He is to have a special care for the outcast and needy; and to those who turn to God he is to declare the forgiveness of sins (The *Ordinal* of the Church of England).

This certainly makes clear the bishop's relation to the Gospel.

The historical succession of bishops in particular places is a powerful sign of the unity of the Church but it has to be set in the larger context of the transmission of what is often called apostolic tradition. Through history there has also been a continuing witness to the faith and practice of the apostles, to the proclamation and application of the Gospel in different places to fulfil different needs, to the celebration of the sacraments of Baptism and the Lord's Supper, to ministries of education, serving the poor and needy, healing the sick, and to communion in prayer and suffering. In other words, the succession of bishops as a sign of unity is not to be isolated from the larger concept of the transmission of the apostolic and catholic faith. We make a mistake if we put too much emphasis on the historical succession of bishops and undervalue the continuity of faith and practice of all Christians through the centuries. On the other hand, we undervalue the way in which Christ has led his Church through history if we entirely ignore or only give partial recognition to the historic episcopate. Thus Anglicans are right, when taking part in ecumenical discussions with Protestant denominations graciously to insist that in any scheme for Church unity the episcopate must be preserved, howbeit in a renewed form.

There have been three basic views of the nature of the historic episcopate within the Anglican Communion. Each of these has advocates today. They are usually expressed with the help of three Latin phrases. The first is that the historic episcopate is of the *esse* (true and necessary being) of the Church. This means that the Church cannot exist in any meaningful way across space and through time without the historic order of bishops. The latter guarantees the Church; all the authority from Christ comes through the episcopate which is the divinely ordained channel of grace. The episcopate has delegated some of its functions to the ordained priesthood and some to the Church as a whole. But the historic episcopate alone is fundamental for the life of the Church. Effectively this means that Protestant denominations are not in fact parts of the one, holy, catholic and apostolic Church. This approach claims too much for the episcopate and is unrealistic about the genuine Christianity of the denominations which do not have the episcopate. It is an erroneous view.

The second is that the episcopate is of the *bene esse* (the well being) of the Church. If the first view has been traditionally associated with dogmatic Anglo-Catholicism (and deriving from traditional Roman Catholicism), then this second view has been associated with dogmatic Evangelicalism or Latitudinarianism (and deriving from traditional Protestantism or rationalism). Episcopacy as the *bene esse* of the Church means that when it is properly functioning in governing and leading of the Church it is a good thing and perhaps the best way of leading the Church. But the Church can effectively be the Church of God without bishops, as is proved, it is said, in Presbyterianism, Lutheranism, Methodism and amongst Baptist churches. This approach does not claim enough for the historic episcopate since it undervalues the particular function that Christ the Lord has given to the episcopate to be the living sign of unity.

The third approach is that episcopacy is of the *plene esse* (fullness of being) of the Church. This view affirms that it is God's perfect will for the Church that it be led by bishops, and takes its inspiration from Ephesians 4:10–13. The historic episcopate has important pastoral functions (as the *bene esse* view allows) as well as theological importance (as the *esse* view overstates). It provides the full embodiment of the Gospel in church order. First of all the historic episcopate provides the effectual sign of unity and, therefore, it embodies in church order the Biblical proclamation that Christ's Church is truly one. Secondly, it embodies in practical church order the principle of apostolicity. The episcopally ordained ministry is both 'sent by God to represent Christ to his Church and functions as representative of that Church. It acts as guardian of the Word and Sacraments, of the faith, and the flock of Christ. The historical order of bishops is, therefore, an effectual sign of the relation of Christ to his Church: for it manifests his authority within and care for the Church. As long as the one Church of God is divided on earth the historic Episcopate can never be a full expression and effective sign of the principles of unity and apostolicity. So the *plene esse* view points us to the future when, in the union of the present churches, the order of bishops will function as God wills that it should. Meanwhile Anglicans should highly value the historic episcopate without claiming too much or too little for it. And they should remember that to present the historic episcopate as belonging to the *plene esse* of the Church is the view to which the Anglican commitment to Scripture, tradition and reason points us.

Talk of *esse, bene esse,* and *plene esse* has been criticized as both majoring on only one aspect of the place of bishops in the Church and of being too metaphysical and theoretical. We are reminded that what is important is the *episcope* which the *episcopos* should exercise. That is, the bishop is to exercise spiritual and moral oversight and leadership in the Church. As we noted earlier, this was possible in primitive times when a bishop was effectively the pastor of one congregation (or cluster of congregations). He knew his flock intimately and was able in Christ's name to be their Shepherd. But with the growth of the size of dioceses the *episcopos* found it difficult effectively to exercise any genuine *episcope!* Further, the historic episcopate became prone to corruption. The document entitled *The Historic Episcopate* produced by the Lambeth Conference of 1930, has the following paragraph:

> In the course of time the Episcopate was greatly affected by secular forces which bent it to many purposes alien to its true character, and went far to obscure its spiritual purpose. It is hard to recognise the successors of the Apostles in the feudal Prelates of the medieval Church, or in the 'peers spiritual' of eighteenth-century England. Moreover, the essential character of the Episcopate was distorted by the development of Papal Supremacy. Such deviations from its true principle are mainly responsible for the general abandonment of Episcopacy by the Protestant churches. The Historic Episcopate as we understand it goes behind the perversions of history to the original conception of the Apostolic Ministry.

While many of the unacceptable aspects of, and accretions to, episcopacy have been removed in the Anglican Communion, there is still the fact of the size of the diocese over which the bishop has pastoral care.

It is true that there are a few small dioceses in which a bishop can truly function as pastor as did the bishops in the early centuries. But we need to emphasize that, because God has given us the historic episcopate which we hold in trust, we have a duty to see that bishops function as apostolic men who are committed to Christ and his Gospel. This may well mean creating smaller dioceses and setting bishops free from a lot of the administrative and committee work in which many seem to spend so much time. We are called by God to create the situation in which bishops as personal signs of the unity of the Church across space and through time, truly live by the Gospel they proclaim, and who, furthermore, exercise genuine *episcope* over the flock that they know well. If this were to occur then the whole concept of ministry — of the priest, deacon, and laity — would probably have to change and change for the better!

The Liturgy of the Eucharist

The origin of the Eucharist is to be traced to the Last Supper recorded by three of the evangelists (Matt. 26:26–29; Mk. 14:22–

25; Lk. 22:14–20) and by St. Paul (1 Cor. 11:23–25), and, secondly, to the meals which the Lord Jesus had with his disciples
after his resurrection. In the early centuries a basic structure developed with recognized contents, variable from place to place.
In the revision of Liturgy in modern times, care has been taken
to try to recover insights from this primitive and formative period
of the Church. It will perhaps be helpful to list the elements of
the liturgy of the Eucharist which are now generally recognized
as necessary in order of the Church truly to fulfil its calling in
celebrating the Eucharist as the primary act of worship on each
Lord's Day. (See *Baptism, Eucharist and Ministry* W.C.C., 1982.)

1. Hymns of praise.
2. An act of repentance.
3. The declaration of God's forgiveness.
4. The reading of the Scriptures and proclamation of the Word
   of God.
5. The confession of the Faith of the Church (Nicene Creed).
6. Prayers of intercession for the Church and the world.
7. The preparation of bread and wine.
8. Thanksgiving to the Father for the creation and redemption
   of the world by Christ.
9. The recital of the words of institution of the Lord's Supper
   from the New Testament.
10. The memorial (*anamnesis*) of the great act of redemption
    which God accomplished through Christ — his passion, death
    and resurrection.
11. The invocation (*epiklesis*) of the Holy Spirit in order that He,
    as the Spirit of Christ, will ensure the real presence of Christ
    with his people and in the sacrament.
12. The dedication and consecration of the worshippers to God.
13. A joining in worship in the communion of saints with God's
    Church triumphant in heaven.
14. Prayer for the Second Coming of Christ to inaugurate the
    Kingdom of God.
15. The Amen of the congregation.
16. The recital of the Lord's Prayer.
17. A sign of reconciliation one to another (the 'Peace').
18. The breaking of the bread.
19. Eating and drinking with one another in communion with
    Christ.
20. A further act of praise.

21. The benediction and the sending out to do God's will in the world.

Here there is a richness in word and symbol which satisfies the deep needs of the human heart for worship and for receiving God's grace.

Bearing all this in mind, it is useful to think of the Eucharist under several aspects, while recognizing that it is one service of worship, made up of different but related parts. The Eucharist (from *eucharistia* = thanksgiving) is a proclamation and celebration of the work of God in creation and redemption, and therefore a great thanksgiving to the Father for all he has done and is doing. It is a uniting with the adoration, praise and thanksgiving which Christ himself as our Representative continually offers to the Father in heaven for us. The Eucharist is a sacrifice of praise and thanksgiving offered in and through Christ. Secondly, the Eucharist is an *anamnesis* (memorial or remembrance) of Christ, the living and effective sign of the sacrifice of Christ, accomplished once for all on the Cross of Calvary. As this unique sacrifice is recalled, Christ, himself, now the living Lord, is present through the Spirit in order to enter into communion with those who make memorial. And in union with the living Lord, who comes to us bearing the marks of his passion, our prayers of intercession arise to the Father, purified and offered by Christ himself.

In the third place, the Eucharist includes the invocation of the Holy Spirit. The presence of Christ is obviously the center of the worship, and the promise of Christ contained in the words of institution ('This is my body . . . my blood') is of fundamental importance to the celebration. We believe that Christ is really and truly present through the Spirit, who is the bond of love who unites us to Christ.

Fourthly, the Eucharist is the communion of the faithful. Christ nourishes the life of his flock as the faithful enjoy communion with him. The sharing of the one bread and the common cup demonstrates, and actually brings into reality (through the Spirit of Christ) the oneness of those who share with Christ. It is in the Eucharist that the fellowship of God's people is fully revealed. Finally, the Eucharist is the meal of the kingdom of God, pointing us to the feast of the future kingdom of God in the life of the age to come. Because the Eucharist is all this — and more — those who participate are strengthened for, and empowered to undertake, God's mission in the world. So at the end of the worship the dismissal sends the worshippers to 'go in peace and serve the Lord'.

A mark of Catholicity is the worship of God through the eucharistic liturgy. Fundamental to the structure, content and ethos of the developed Eucharist celebrated in the Church over the centuries is the doctrine of Christ presented in the Nicene Creed (itself usually recited in the Liturgy). This doctrine includes both the coming of God to the human race, and the taking of our humanity to the Father in and by the one Christ. It is imperative for the right use and understanding of the eucharistic liturgy that we hold not only to the idea of the *descent* of the eternal Son of God, but also to his *ascent* with our human nature. The human nature that he made his own in the womb of the Virgin Mary has become the vicarious humanity which he now has in heaven. Without his vicarious humanity our worship loses significance. Our exalted Lord is in heaven as our Priest before the Father and he is perpetually offering perfect worship to the Father arising from perfect love and trust. Christian worship is to worship in such a way that we accept the gift of participation through the Spirit of Christ in the communion of the exalted Jesus with the Father. Our worship is not only through our Lord Jesus but also in him, in his vicarious humanity. He is certainly the Mediator between God and man; but, he is also our Priest and Representative and we are included in him, as the Second Adam. As we allow the Spirit to lead us so that in union with Christ we are united to his self offering to, and worship of, the Father, then our adoration, praise and thanksgiving is perfect in his worthy worship of the Father, and our intercessions for the Church and the world are joined to his heavenly intercession.

Our Liturgy works on this understanding of Christ as our Priest and thus we are invited to share in Christ's heavenly worship through our union with, and in, him. Let us recall the old *Sursum Corda:*

> Lift up your hearts.
> We lift them up unto the Lord.

Here there is the clear intention of sharing in the worship that already is being offered in heaven. So a little later come the words, 'Therefore with angels and archangels and all the company of heaven, we laud and magnify thy glorious name' (*The Book of Common Prayer*). The modern eucharistic services are more explicit.

Accept through him, our great high priest
this our sacrifice of thanks and praise;
and as we eat and drink these holy gifts
in the presence of your divine majesty,
renew us by your Spirit,
inspire us with your love,
and unite us in the body of your Son,
Jesus Christ our Lord.

Through him and with him, and in him,
by the power of the Spirit,
with all who stand before you in earth
    and heaven,
we worship you, Father almighty,
in songs of everlasting praise.
(*Alternative Service Book,* 1980)

The key words are 'through . . . with . . . in' the exalted Lord,
that is in his vicarious humanity.

This approach to worship is the way of grace, the way that
proceeds from the Gospel. It releases within the worshippers great
joy, love and peace. For, as we are lifted out of ourselves by the
Spirit of Christ into Christ himself, we are blessed by the Father
in Christ. This is worship that is truly in spirit and in truth for it is
participation in Christ's communion with the Father. 'Truly our
fellowship is with the Father and with his Son' (1 John 1:3).

Regrettably, though written into the Liturgy, this approach to
worship has not been as prominent as it ought to have been in
the Anglican Communion. Far too many of us think of worship
as if it were something that we do in our own power in the
church building on Sundays. We view worship as that activity in
which we engage by arriving, by kneeling, by sitting, by standing,
by singing, by taking bread and wine, and so on. We do it sincerely and reverently as our duty to God, Creator and Redeemer.
In fact we really try our best. But the problem with this approach
is that it is *our* worship, *our* doing, *our* effort and *our* activity. It
effectively denies that Christ is our Priest in heaven and that we
are dependent upon him. It leads to weariness, boredom, frustra-
tion and meaninglessness.

In order to recover a genuine Catholicity in worship we need
to recover fully the true doctrine and ethos of the Eucharist. Only
by so doing, and by allowing the Spirit of the exalted Lord to
cause us to share in the worship of Christ, will we know the
Liturgy truly to be divine Liturgy, that experience in which we

come to the Father through and in the Son and from the Father receive the heavenly benediction.

The truth is that we neglect the vicarious humanity of our Saviour and deny the Gospel if we seek to worship in our own power. We also effectively deny the vicarious humanity of Christ if we substitute for it the vicarious humanity of the Virgin Mary, the saints and martyrs. The latter has been done by Roman Catholics and Anglo-Catholics and is an error. To join with the company of heaven and in the communion of saints is right and proper and a joy: but we must remember that the salvation of that company is wholly dependent upon Christ, the exalted Saviour—even the Virgin Mary worships the Father through, and in, her Son. She needs that vicarious humanity which he actually took from her. The true catholic way is the way of the Gospel of the grace of God and the way of the vicarious humanity of Christ.

Visible Unity

Perhaps in the West we have gotten so used to the idea of different and competitive Christian denominations that the scandal of the disunity of the one Church of God rarely strikes us. We see it from our childhood and it becomes a part of the regular scenery. For several centuries Protestantism has divided and subdivided and this has left the Christian Church presenting itself today as the accumulation of hundreds of denominations. And, let us admit, that even as competition between commercial companies causes them to be more committed in the way they trade, so it would appear that competition between denominations within a town does in a strange way actually help them to get on with their task of mission, evangelism and social service. So we can provide pragmatic arguments for the continuance of denominational rivalry and avoid serious thought and discussion of the concept of the unity of the Church.

Furthermore, many of us are rarely impressed by the statements from, and the activities promoted by, the World Council of Churches from the Geneva office. Also the long and tedious negotiations, which appear to happen when denominational bureaucrats and long-worded theologians talk about unity, seem to be ineffectual and so far from reality. And even when our ecumenical negotiators appear to find a successful agreement in terms of ways forward, their proposals are not always treated with enthusiasm at the grass-roots level. Instead of being keen to promote a real, visible unity, many of us are half-hearted and do not want to think too seriously about it — despite the prayers we offer in the Week of Prayer for Christian Unity. We dismiss it either on pragmatic or, sometimes, on dogmatic grounds.

The most common dogmatic ground on which visible unity is rejected as a goal is that the true unity of the Church is, and was meant only to be, spiritual and invisible. God alone sees it as a whole and welcomes it as a whole. In this way of thinking, common among evangelicals, the 'one, holy, catholic and apostolic Church' is presented as being the total number, known only to God, who are born again. This is the true, invisible Church. And while members of this Church will normally be members of a visible, local church, it does not follow that each member of a local church is a member of the invisible, true Church. Thus it is argued that to work for unity is a waste of energy; it is far better to use that energy to add to the number of the true, invisible Church. We must be realistic and live with competitive denominations and societies.

Catholic-minded Christians who are gripped by the Evangel, must seek not to allow either pragmatic or supposed dogmatic views to reduce their commitment to the will of God on earth. While it is true that God alone knows his elect, it is also true that his will is that the Church is to be a visible unity on earth, so that it may testify to his reconciling love. Unity does not mean uniformity; but unity does ultimately require that in each locality there be only one true church serving Christ in that area, and that such a local church be in fellowship with similar churches in surrounding areas, and that the churches (= Church) of one country be in fellowship with the churches (= Church) of other countries.

Of course, in any growth toward unity there would be intermediate positions in which several churches in the one specific area found ways of growing together first into eucharistic and then into organic communion. The aim must be to come to the situation in which there is one worshipping and witnessing congregation in one area and that the scandal of competitive churches be removed. Such a local church would have a variety of ways of worship, of forms of ministry and expressions of mission, but it would be one church and one fellowship. Naturally in a town or city there would be an association of such churches, with perhaps a central one being regarded as 'the first among equals'. We do not know precisely how the Lord would guide us if our hearts and wills were truly motivated by Christ's desire for the unity of his people.

In the high priestly prayer of Jesus there are definite indications that God wills the unity of the Church on earth: 'I pray that they may all be one. Father! May they be in us, just as you are in me and I am in you. May they be one, so that the world will believe that you sent me. I gave them the same glory you gave me, so that they may be one, just as you and I are one: I in them and you in me, so that they may be completely one, in order that the world may know that you sent me and that you love them as you love me' (John 17:21–23 TEV). The mission of the Church in and to the world is adversely affected unless there is genuine unity among those who follow Jesus. Writing to the Ephesians St. Paul wrote that 'there is one body and one Spirit, just as there is one hope to which God has called you. There is one Lord, one faith, one baptism; there is one God and Father of all mankind, who is Lord of all, works through all, and is in all' (Eph. 4:4–6 TEV).

Anglicans presuppose this unity when they pray in the Eucharist: 'We humbly beseech thee . . . to inspire continually the universal Church with the spirit of truth, unity and concord, and grant that all they that do confess thy holy name may agree in the truth of thy holy word and live in unity and godly love' (*The Book of Common Paryer*). Then in the modern Litany we pray: 'Govern and direct your holy Church; fill it with love and truth; and grant it that unity which is your will'.

In the light of the known will of God for the visible unity of the Church, our commitment to Catholicity requires that we do all within our power to grow together with other Christians towards unity in Christ. The best place to start is in the local diocese and parish. Here ways, appropriate for that locality, can be developed to enable Christians from different traditions to meet and grow together in and towards Christ. Where there is a large variety of local churches (from Roman Catholic through Greek Orthodox to Methodist, Presbyterian and Baptist) this would appear to be an impossible calling from God. Our only comfort is that Christ is on our side (because we are on his) if we pray and work for that unity which is gospel-centered. There is such a chasm between some local Christian groups that only as Christ leads is there any hope of reconciliation in him. Further, the speed of local growth toward unity will both affect and be affected by what is achieved by the interdenominational commissions on unity. Certainly, too, many unity schemes have been too top heavy and have had little support at the grass roots. Thus we have to find the right combination of activity both at the grass roots and denominational level. And leadership in each particular Church or denomination is important — think of the beneficial effects of the Second Vatican Council.

In the two gospel-sacraments we already have signs of visible unity, even though baptism is the only one of the two which is universally accepted as valid. Baptism is incorporation into Christ and it is also incorporation into his Church, which includes into the local church as the microcosm of the whole. If there are competitive congregations in one locality, then the full meaning of this sacrament of initiation is obscured or its efficacy hampered. The Eucharist presupposes that there is one local expression of the Body of Christ for all share in one bread and one cup. It makes little sense for several Eucharists to be celebrated at the same time by competitive (or even sympathetic) congregations if the sacrament is the sacrament of unity.

Then, as Anglicans, we are to take seriously the historic episcopate as the sign of the unity of the Church in space and time. The order of bishops cannot guarantee unity; but, those of us who are united together around a bishop have a particular duty to pray and work, in charity and with humility, for the visible unity of all local Christians around that episcopate. To believe in bishops is to be committed to the visible unity of the people of God.

It is possible for an individual to get so obsessed with the methods and management of the ecumenical exercise that he or she becomes an ecumaniac. Perhaps you have met such a person. The argument being offered here is that, if the Anglican Church is rising to the call to be wholly evangelical and wholly catholic, then, as part of its total life and experience, it will do all within its power to work towards visible unity. If the pursuit of unity is undertaken in a spirit that is similar to the promotion of a new commercial product, then it will only generate further division and hostility. The pursuit of visible unity is to be the result of the commitment of the people of God to the Gospel and to Catholicity. Unless the growth towards unity occurs on this foundation, and within this ethos, it will have very little spiritual momentum and minimum effect upon the divided people of God. The potential of the Anglican Communion to serve the Lord as a catalyst and promotor of unity has only rarely been allowed to function. We must remedy this sin of omission.

As long ago as 1888 the Lambeth Conference adopted (from the General Convention of the Protestant Episcopal Church held in Chicago in 1886) four statements known as the *Lambeth Quadrilateral*. They state the basic essentials for a united Church, as perceived from an Anglican viewpoint:

A. The Holy Scriptures of the Old and New Testaments as 'containing all things necessary to salvation' and as being the rule and ultimate standard of faith.

B. The Apostles' Creed, as the Baptismal Symbol; and the Nicene Creed, as the sufficient statement of the Christian Faith.

C. The two Sacraments as ordained by Christ himself — Baptism and the Supper of the Lord — ministered with unfailing use of Christ's Word of Institution, and of the elements ordained by him.

D. The Historic Episcopate, locally adapted in the methods of its administration to the varying needs of the nations and people called of God into the Unity of his Church.

Rightly viewed this *Quadrilateral* should function as a symbol of the fulness of genuine Catholic tradition. The appeal to the Scriptures points to the recovery of a biblically-based faith in the living God, our Creator, Redeemer and Judge. It also points to the living and exalted Lord Jesus, Viceregent of the Father, and to the Holy Spirit, the Paraclete and Sanctifier of the Church. The appeal to the Creeds directs the Church in its understanding of the Gospel and Scriptures while the appeal to the two Sacraments, together with the Creeds, keeps before us the great tradition of evangelism, mission and corporate worship over the centuries. Finally the order of bishops is presented in such a way as to include the appeal to primitive times when bishops were responsible for only one congregation or a small cluster of congregations. This allows for different developments of episcopacy in different places and cultures.

A Compelling Vision

Where there is no vision the people perish. To serve God, the divided Church, and to engage in God's mission to the world, the Anglican Communion needs to be inspired by a vision. It needs a goal. What we have offered as the general shape of that vision has appeared under the twin themes of the Evangel and Catholicity. In this epilogue there is need to state more clearly (but not over precisely or else the vision will become a scheme or plan) the nature of the vision.

Perhaps it will be helpful to state first of all what the vision is not.

1. It is not the realization of a *via media* in the sense of being a middle way between Roman Catholicism and Protestant Evangelicalism. The vision is certainly not to provide a way that has one foot within traditional Protestantism and the other within Roman Catholicism. Such a way would be a nightmare! The Church of England was never intended to be such a society by the Elizabethan Settlement (1559) and Anglicanism is not called to be such a movement.

2. It is not a synthesis of existing schools of thought and churchmanship within Anglicanism. The vision is not a creative combination of the positive elements in the Evangelical, Anglo-Catholic and Liberal/Radical approaches.

3. It is not being wholly catholic in liturgy and order and wholly evangelical in preaching and theology.

4. It is not a movement from the present position of compromise to the total way, in the sense that there will be a union of seemingly opposite principles.

5. It is not the holding together various aspects of truth in a healthy tension so that the Anglican Communion can fulfil a

special vocation to be a mediator and bridge builder in the ecumenical movement.

6. It is not even the creation of a kind of ecclesial symbiosis (symbiosis being the permanent union between organisms, each of which is dependent for its existence on the other) in which the Gospel and Catholicity live off, and feed on, each other.

While there is truth in most of these ways of looking at the vocation of Anglicanism, the vision is not conveyed by any of them, or by a combination of some of them. Rather it is that the key to the union of the true Gospel and genuine Catholicity is in the one, resurrected and ascended Lord Jesus, who is our Prophet, Priest and King, and who makes himself known to us in and by the Spirit.

Union with the exalted Lord at any point in space and time implies, and requires, a constant and wholehearted commitment to the Gospel, of which he is Creator and Center, as well as to the historical continuing Church of which he is the Creator, Lord and Life-Giver. Only as we allow our eyes to be lifted up to view our exalted Lord, and only as we allow our hearts and wills to follow the gaze of our eyes, will we be able to see, in their correct relation, the Evangel and the Catholic Church and Faith. Christ is the same yesterday, today and forever; he calls the Anglican Communion, and each part of it, as they are united to God through, with and in him, to be wholly evangelical and wholly catholic. Growth in and toward Christ will cause us to see, as very secondary, our loyalties to parties, personalities and causes, for he is the Alpha and the Omega, and the One in whom all things find their ultimate meaning. This is surely a compelling vision which can, and should, be realized in our generation.

And it is given added weight when we remember that we are called to watch and to pray because our exalted Lord will return to earth 'to judge the living and the dead'. In the mood of watching and praying the commitment to the Evangel and Catholicity can be perfectly expressed. So let us begin immediately to implement the vision — each of us in the parish and the bishop in his diocese.

High-Church Evangelical
and Evangelical High-Churchman

In 1833 the Tractarian, or Oxford, or Anglo-Catholic Movement was born. Those within this movement went further in their commitment to, and enthusiasm for, patristic and medieval principles, practice and spirituality than the traditional High-Church school had ever done. And, fear that the leaders — John Henry Newman, John Keble and Edward B. Pusey — and their disciples/friends were seeking to restore major aspects of imbalanced or erroneous medieval worship and doctrine in the Church of England caused not only the traditional Evangelicals but also other Churchmen, including High Churchmen, to express misgivings and concern. By 1840 a major controversy had begun and it continued throughout the Victorian period. (For details see my *Evangelical Theology: A Response to Tractarianism,* John Knox Press, 1979.)

As the division between Anglo-Catholics and Evangelicals widened in the 1840's there were those from the Evangelical and High-Church Schools who believed that the extremes of their positions — as exhibited in the controversy — were unacceptable and denied the Reformed Catholicity of the Church of England. So a few men chose to call themselves Evangelical High-Churchmen or High-Church Evangelicals. The particular name reflected the route taken toward the position and also reflected the particular way that Reformed Catholicity was expressed. There was a common conviction that the Church of England already had a Reformed or Evangelical Catholicity and should not exaggerate its evangelical or its catholic nature in such a manner as to detract from the dynamic nature of Reformed Catholicity.

Those who sought to take this position of affirming what was true in each of the contesting positions were only a minority. The magazine and publications in which they expressed their convictions did not last long. Their influence was minimal in their own time and the Church of England apparently soon forgot about them. (See further my article 'Evangelicals and Tractarians: then and now' in *The Churchman*, 1979.)

It was (and is) so much easier to adopt one neatly packaged position or expression of Anglican Christianity than to seek to affirm and to hold truths expressed in various packages. There is nothing wrong in belonging to a School (better than the word 'party'), but the major commitment of the Anglican Christian is to the exalted Lord Jesus and to his whole Church. Schools of thought and practice should exist as complementary expressions of the one Faith and one commitment to the Lord Jesus, just as a variety of ministries needs to exist to complement one another and to point to the one ministry of Christ himself. Unity, without uniformity, is the right idea.

The continuance of the genuine 'Liberal' or 'Latitudinarian' School has a place in the Anglican Way that is simultaneously evangelical and catholic. To this School belongs the task of constantly bringing before the whole Church the kinds of questions it should be facing, and of constantly pioneering new ways of thinking about Faith and about the relations of the Faith and Church to the world in which they are set. Yet this questioning and creative thinking will be done in faithfulness to the Gospel and to Catholicity.

To put the matter simply, I see in the Anglican Way those who are EVANGELICAL and catholic, those who are CATHOLIC and evangelical, and those who are LIBERAL, evangelical and catholic (or LIBERAL, catholic and evangelical) — together with other possible permutations. The point is that together, as a body, we shall reflect and exhibit a simultaneous commitment to the Gospel and Catholicity.

Radical Theology and Comprehensiveness

The pursuit of the study of theology in universities (especially in Europe) and seminaries (especially in America) is often minimally related to the faith, life, work, witness and worship of the congregations of Christians in our parishes. Within the intellectual atmosphere of the secular university/seminary, the study of theology can so easily be removed from the life of prayer and the way of worship, and placed instead within the terms of reference of academia (which no longer sees theology as the queen of the sciences). There is little doubt that this fact makes many ordinary Christian people suspicious of 'academic' theologians and fearful of their latest and brightest ideas.

Let us be clear. There are all kinds of beneficial results which arise from the study of theology in the secular ethos of academia. Intellectual rigor is brought to bear in all departments of our thinking from biblical exegesis through church history to moral theology. Further, there is already perception of the big questions which we must face as Christians if we are to be able to claim that our faith has meaning and relevance in the scientific era and technological age.

But there are also dangers. These arise mostly from the fact that Christian minds — often of priests — are set free (within the secularized influence of academia) from their association with what the Church has always believed, taught and confessed to begin to look for new ways of explaining the fact and importance of Jesus, or the nature of Christianity for our modern world. The 'controls' of prayer, worship and the fellowship of Christians are absent (or not prominent) and so the speculation and desire to produce novel ideas increase. Further, before these novel ideas are tested and debated within the lecture halls and seminar rooms of the academic institution, they are sometimes written down and published (regrettably, by so-called Christian publishers) as 'the latest important advances in theology'. And so often, they are the undigested and untested secularized thoughts of well-meaning academics who are trying hard to produce novel hypotheses concerning one or another aspect of theology.

Of course, there is good in these books and they do help us to recognize the questions that are being asked, and ought to be asked, in our generation. But the point is that this negative, radical theology (which usually denies basic Trinitarianism and classic Christology) does not help the Church at all, in the long term, to be the committed people of God in word and deed in the world. This kind of negative theology neither increases loyalty to the Gospel nor commitment to Catholicity. Further, after being much publicized these radical theologies usually disappear or are quietly forgotten.

If academics in the university wish to advance hypotheses which challenge or deny the long-held claims of the Church then they are free to do that within their lectures, seminars and books. But the Church in its role as the 'pillar and bulwark of the truth' has a duty to watch over the faith and to guard it against those who would deny it. So we do need to prevent priests who have adopted negative, radical theologies from teaching in our church-related seminaries, where, let us not forget, the future teachers of the faithful are being prepared for ministry. We do need to ask our Christian publishing houses not to add to the confusion of the faithful by producing what are obviously (by traditional standards) heretical books. The faithful need to arise from their pews and let their voices be heard calling for a dynamic and vital Christian faith — true to orthodoxy and facing the world of today — to be taught in our seminaries and proclaimed within our churches. Seminaries should be communities of prayer, worship and fellowship in which theology is pursued so that faith is in search of understanding — credo ut intelligam (I believe in order to understand). Let the students arise and call for their seminaries to be such places. I am not calling for witch-hunts or for heresy trials. The sound Anglican Way is the way of gentle, but firm persuasion, with a compassion for the people involved. Further, I am not calling for dead orthodoxy, which delights in the concepts and language of earlier centuries. The sound Anglican Way is the way of theology and practice which is faithful to yesterday and today, but not dominated by yesterday.